Spiritual Cleansing

The Ultimate Guide to Psychic Protection, Reiki, Ways to Cleanse Your Chakras, Auras, and Raising Your Vibration

Your Free Gift
(only available for a limited time)

Thanks for getting this book! If you want to learn more about various spirituality topics, then join Mari Silva's community and get a free guided meditation MP3 for awakening your third eye. This guided meditation mp3 is designed to open and strengthen ones third eye so you can experience a higher state of consciousness. Simply visit the link below the image to get started.

https://spiritualityspot.com/meditation

Table of Contents

Introduction

Are you searching for ways to protect yourself from negative energy and raise your vibration? If so, you've come to the right place. In this ultimate guide to spiritual cleansing, you will learn the basics of psychic protection, how to use Reiki to send healing energy, how to cleanse and balance your chakras, clear negative energy from your aura, and raise your vibration to a higher frequency. Comprising of 10 thoroughly researched and expertly vetted chapters on all things spiritual, following the advice in this insightful book will empower you to protect yourself from negative energy and live a life of positive vibes.

Chapter one (You and Your Spiritual Welfare) will enlighten you on the significance of spiritual cleansing and welfare. It answers commonly asked questions, including:

- Why should I care about my spiritual welfare?
- Why must I learn to spiritually cleanse and protect myself or my home? What am I cleansing or protecting myself from?
- How do I know I'm cleansed and protected?
- Can anyone practice spiritual cleansing?
- And more

Through this, you will learn valuable skills to improve your quality of life and clear your mind. By examining what chakras are, where they come from, their purpose, and why they are essential, chapter two (Your Aura and Chakras 101) provides an overview of how energy flows through life forces. It gets more in-depth about each chakras symbol, their Sanskrit names, origins, location, and how they can influence you. You learn about your aura for good health, vitality, and a positive attitude.

Once you understand how your mind and body connect, chapter three (Cleansing Your Aura and Chakras) will teach you how to clear and unblock each chakra and cleanse your aura. It will get you well on the way to happiness and peace. Chapter four (Meditation to Raise Your Vibration) provides insight into vibrational frequency and how it can help you emotionally. You will discover clear, actionable, step-by-step instructions for a simple meditation exercise to raise your vibration and many more valuable tips for busy people.

Chapter 5 (The Healing Power of Reiki) introduces you to the power of Reiki, how it works, and how you can use it to your advantage. There are plenty of tips and tricks for how to put things into practice and apply them to your life. Don't worry if you're not familiar with the concept of Reiki, as the practice is thoroughly explained. Chapter six (Cleansing Energy with Reiki) gets a little more exciting with hands-on, practical exercises to clear unwanted energy through several Reiki techniques. You will learn about smudging in chapter seven (To Smudge or Not to Smudge) and why some consider this cleansing method controversial. Nonetheless, there are plenty of illustrations and clear instructions on creating your smudge stick from accessible herbs. Then, you can use smudging to cleanse yourself, the home, and other people or objects.

How is a spiritual bath different from any other bath? This question is answered in chapter eight (Spiritual Baths for Cleansing and Protection). You will discover the benefits of spiritual bathing and some creative recipes with ingredients and clear step-by-step instructions for creating a spiritual bath for cleansing and protection. In chapter nine (Crystal Purification and Protection), crystals and stones are discussed as cleansing and protection methods. A comprehensive list of various crystals you can use, and their spiritual meanings are included.

Once you've learned how to cleanse and protect yourself, you are shown how to keep others spiritually safe, wherever they are, in chapter ten (Cleansing and Protecting Your Loved Ones). The book closes with a detailed glossary of useful spiritual cleansing herbs.

Chapter 1: You and Your Spiritual Welfare

Spiritual cleansing is an integral part of maintaining your mental and emotional welfare. It is the purification of your spirit and energy field so you become more connected to your higher self and the divine essence surrounding you. Through this journey, you reconnect with your inner wisdom, gain clarity on life's challenges, and open your heart to greater joy and contentment. By engaging in metaphysical cleansing, you'll discover insight into your life's purpose and a greater sense of peace and well-being. This chapter walks you through this robust process so you can create balance and harmony within yourself and your life and release any negative energy preventing you from achieving your highest potential.

Your spiritual welfare should always be a priority.
https://pxhere.com/en/photo/1394621

The Importance of Spiritual Welfare

Spiritual welfare is the foundation of a healthy and fulfilling life. It encompasses the well-being of the mind, body, and soul and is essential to achieve inner peace and happiness. The importance of spiritual welfare cannot be overstated, as it is crucial in shaping your thoughts, feelings, and actions.

Pursuing spiritual welfare involves developing a solid connection with your inner self and a higher power or force governing the universe. Through it, you gain direction and meaning in life and understand the reason for your existence. When spiritually fulfilled, you are better equipped to deal with the challenges and complexities of life. You are more resilient and can handle stress and adversity better. Besides that, spiritual welfare is closely linked to your physical and mental health. Research in the *Journal of Happiness Studies* shows that spiritually fulfilled people are more likely to have a positive outlook on life and are less prone to depression and anxiety. They have lower levels of stress hormones in their bodies, reducing the risk of developing chronic illnesses, such as heart disease, diabetes, and cancer. Spiritual welfare cultivates virtues like compassion, forgiveness, and gratitude. These qualities are essential to build strong and fulfilling relationships with others and create community and belonging. They encourage you to be more empathetic and understanding toward others and to see the world from different perspectives.

Ultimately, spiritual welfare is vital to lead a fulfilling and meaningful life. It enriches your life, provides a purpose, makes coping with stress and adversity easier, and promotes physical and mental well-being. You can lead a more joyful, compassionate, and productive life by prioritizing your spiritual welfare.

Spiritual Cleansing Promotes Spiritual Welfare

Spiritual cleansing is an ancient practice used for centuries to clear the mind, body, and spirit of negative energy. Its origins can be traced to various cultures and religions, including Hinduism, Buddhism, and Native American traditions.

- In Hinduism, spiritual cleansing is called *"shuddhi,"* which includes using mantras, meditation, and yoga.
- Spiritual cleansing in Buddhism is known as "purity of mind," the practice of mindfulness, meditation, and self-reflection.
- Native American traditions have unique spiritual cleansing methods, including smudging with sage, sweetgrass, or cedar.

In each method, negative energy, emotions, and thoughts are removed and replaced with positive energy.

Reasons Your Well-Being Needs a Pick-Me-Up

Spiritual pollution is an interesting concept to explore and can profoundly impact your life. It's worth taking a step back to look at contamination of the spirit and how it happens. At its core, pollution of inner health is environmental turmoil affecting spiritual well-being, and it happens in two ways.

1. Firstly, it can be caused by physical environmental factors, such as pollution, noise, and overcrowding. This toxicity can directly affect mental and emotional well-being, damaging the natural environment and disturbing your peace of mind.

2. The second way spiritual pollution can happen is through more intangible factors, like thoughts, beliefs, and values. This stress is caused by your mental and emotional state. Negative thoughts, beliefs, and values can have an insidious effect on divine connection, as they can gradually erode optimism, gratitude, and relationship with the divine.

Ultimately, spiritual pollution is something everyone needs to be mindful of. Whether physical or psychological in nature, it can devastatingly impact lives. You must be aware of your environment and thoughts and do your best to keep them free of pollution to combat it and ensure your inner health remains strong and vibrant.

How to Know if You Need Spiritual Cleansing

Everyone is exposed to a certain degree of spiritual pollution in their daily lives, through the media, environment, or even their actions. But how do you know when it's time to give your spirit a good cleansing? Here are a few signs indicating it's time to do some soul-searching and cleanse yourself of detrimental influences.

The first sign is a feeling of being stuck. If you feel stuck in a rut and unable to move forward, it may be time to look inward and clear out whatever is holding you back. It could be negative thoughts or ideas, patterns of behavior, or even toxic relationships preventing you from realizing your true potential.

Another sign is physical symptoms like fatigue, headaches, or exhaustion. If you're feeling these physical symptoms and can't shake them, it could be a sign something deeper is occurring, and possibly your spirit is weighed down by harmful energy.

The final sign is feeling disconnected from yourself and your overall purpose. If you're merely going through the motions and not living life to its fullest, it's time to take a step back and purify yourself of your ego. A spiritual cleanse can help clear negative vibrations blocking your connection to your true self and help you reconnect with your higher purpose.

With all this talk of personal wellness, you may wonder if you can use spiritual healing on non-physical things. The answer is absolute, yes. This practice is based on unfavorable energy trapped in a space, creating an atmosphere of fear, sadness, or anger if left unchecked. Purification eliminates this harmful force, creating a more positive and peaceful atmosphere in the home.

Suppose you're experiencing any of the above signs. In that case, it's time to take a step back and give yourself a good cleanse of the soul, reconnect with your true self, and move forward in life with greater clarity and purpose. The good news is anyone can engage in spiritual cleansing. It is not an activity exclusive to a particular religion or belief system. Everyone can benefit from it, regardless of their background. The key to successful metaphysical purification is focusing on yourself and your connection to the natural world.

The Role of Spiritual Cleansing and Welfare

Spiritual cleansing and welfare are concepts that have been around for centuries but have recently become more popular as people become more aware of the power of energy. It is a practice using various rituals, symbols, and techniques to clear negative energy from your life and attract positive energy.

Spiritual Energy

Spiritual energy is the vital force within and around you all the time. It is a power that exists on an energetic level, making it difficult to measure, but it is definitely there. It is the vital force connecting you to the divine world and the power to open you up to your spiritual self and the spiritual bodies of others. It is often described as a life force connected to your soul. This power helps you to become more aware of your inner self and better understand yourself and the world around you. This energy is also connected to your aura, an energetic field surrounding you.

Your aura comprises the divine power within you and helps protect you from outside influences. Energy from the spiritual realm can be used in many different ways, such as healing and manifesting. When used correctly, this divine power becomes a powerful tool to achieve your goals. It is a great way to connect to the spiritual world because it enables more awareness of the subtleties of life that are often taken for granted. By connecting to your spiritual energy, you learn to trust your intuition and use your spiritual energy to manifest what you desire in life.

How Spiritual Cleaning Affects Spiritual Energy

The role of spiritual cleansing and welfare is often misunderstood by many. But ultimately, it is the concept that each person comprises a physical body, a soul, and an aura. The physical body is what you see and feel, the soul is the energy making up your being, and the aura is the energy field surrounding you. Your physical body is as important as your spiritual state of being. Your soul comprises energies that are constantly in motion, and these energies affect physical and mental health.

- **Aura cleansing** is spiritual purification restoring the natural power of the aura, the energy field surrounding your physical body. This aura cleansing helps remove unwelcome or stagnant energy and restores the flow of vitality in the aura. It protects you from detrimental influences affecting your physical, mental, and spiritual well-being.

- **Spiritual welfare** is vital for overall well-being. It is being mindful of your soul's needs and taking steps to ensure you live in harmony with your spiritual self, including engaging in spiritual pursuits like meditation, visualization, and prayer. It is being mindful of your thoughts and feelings and ensuring you live aligned with your highest self.

When spiritually unbalanced, your energy becomes blocked or stagnant, which leads to physical, emotional, and mental issues. The ultimate goal is to foster self-awareness and spiritual growth. You become more in tune with your spiritual self and understand your spiritual needs and desires by clearing negative feelings. It helps you make choices and decisions aligned with your highest good.

Spiritual rejuvenation and welfare are important aspects of well-being. They eliminate negative energy and restore your spiritual body to its natural balance. They encourage being mindful of spiritual needs and assuring harmonious living with your true self. You can clear harmful energies, and engage in activities fostering self-awareness and spiritual growth, leading to increased well-being and balance by engaging in metaphysical exercises.

The Act of Spiritual Cleansing

Spiritual welfare is of utmost importance in today's world. Living in a world of energy, keeping your spiritual energy clean and safe is essential to ensure mental and physical well-being. Learning to detox and spiritually protect yourself or your home is essential to creating protective boundaries with people and situations that bring you down. Whether you are spiritual or not, understanding how to perform spiritual purification can be exceptionally beneficial. Listed below are a few of the many reasons for spiritual cleansing:

- To reduce stress, worry, fear, anger, doubt, or other unpleasant emotions.
- To protect yourself from external influences such as curses, hexes, or other negative energies.
- To increase your mental clarity and focus.
- To bring peace and balance into your life.
- To reduce the physical symptoms of negative energy.
- To improve relationships with others.
- To promote life purpose.
- To boost self-connection.

The main reason is that cleansing your spirit can clear bad vibrations and help you reset your energy levels. When bad energy accumulates in your life, it is hard to focus on the positive and stay in a good headspace. Performing a purifying ritual will clear away this toxic energy, allowing you to move forward with a fresh perspective. Purification will benefit you in times of stress or difficulty, as it provides calm amid the chaos to bring tranquility and peace. In addition, the act will heighten your intuition, allowing you to make better decisions and keep you in tune with your inner voice. Finally, learning to perform a spiritual cleanse connects you more deeply with the spiritual world. You learn to open up to new ideas and insights and connect to a higher power that can provide guidance and wisdom.

What Happens During and After Spiritual Cleansing?

Spiritual cleansing is a powerful process to help clear negative vibrations and reconnect with your higher self. You can open the door to manifesting desires and healing emotional trauma by setting an intention and utilizing various techniques to clear energy blocks. The action begins with an intention to clear unwanted energy blocking your spiritual progress. The best way is by visualizing a white light flowing through your body, washing away all the unwanted vibrations. Other methods include:

- Burning sage or other appropriate herbs
- Crystal healing
- Reciting mantras or affirmations
- Meditation
- Visualization
- Smudging

Once the purification is complete, you should feel lighter, more balanced, and more connected to your higher self.

What Spiritual Cleansing Looks Like

A few key elements are essential for spiritual cleansing and protection.

1. First, you need an open mind. To make the best of spiritual cleansing, you must accept that there are forces beyond what you

can see or hear. It requires a willingness to take a leap of faith and be open to the possibilities existing beyond the physical world.

2. Second, you need a personal connection to the higher world through meditation, prayer, or another spiritual practice. Connecting to the spiritual realm allows you to access the energy and healing power of the spiritual world, to purify and safeguard your life.

3. Third, you need knowledge of spiritual purification and protection techniques. There are many ways to purify and safeguard yourself, and it's important to understand the different techniques and how they work. It allows you to apply the methods to get the most out of them.

4. Finally, you must have patience and focus. The entire endeavor takes time and effort, so it's crucial to have patience and focus to stick with it because it's ultimately worth it. As you develop and refine your technique, you'll use spiritual purification and safeguarding more effectively and efficiently.

Essentially, the healing process is the only way to enhance your well-being.

What a Cleansed Spirit Feels Like

The feeling of being cleansed and protected is difficult to describe, but when you experience it, you'll know. After a good cleanse, you feel an overall sense of peace and well-being. You'll feel an increased clarity that wasn't there before and protection shielding you from the world's negative energies. It's a sensation often described as being enveloped in a bubble of peace and love. You'll experience a heightened awareness of yourself and your surroundings. As you experience this, you become more in tune with your intuition and more connected to the spiritual world. Also, you'll be less affected by the stress and negativity of the world around you and more in touch with your inner power.

Modern life can sometimes be stressful, making it easy to lose your way. Inevitably, there will be days when your cleansing feels weaker than usual, no matter how hard you work to improve yourself. However, you shouldn't worry about this, as it's easy to get back on track because everything you have done up to this point involves tuning into your inner energy, aura, and spirit. All you need to do is reconnect with yourself, usually through meditation. Meditation will clear your mind and help you connect with yourself more deeply. As you meditate, focus on being cleansed and protected. Visualize a protective bubble of light around you, and imagine the loving energy of the universe washing away the negative energy clinging to you. Ultimately, feeling rejuvenated and secure is a unique experience left to individual interpretation. This feeling cannot be forced, so take time to relax and connect with yourself, allowing the feeling to come naturally. Only then will you be closer to becoming the best version of yourself.

Spiritual cleansing is becoming increasingly popular with people of all ages and backgrounds. It's an ancient method to restore balance and harmony to the mind, body, and soul. This process is used for protection and to raise your vibration. It helps clear out stagnant chi, emotional blockages, and negative patterns in your life and is an essential part of spiritual growth and self-care. Use it to open up your spiritual energy channels, create an open and clear association with your higher self, and connect to the divine power within you. Purifying your spirit can be done through various rituals, such as using sage or palo santo to clear negative chi, using crystals or bathing to clear out unwanted energy, or meditation or chanting mantras to raise your vibration. Ultimately, spiritual cleansing is a powerful way to connect with yourself and the divine while providing protection and a higher vibration.

Chapter 2: Your Aura and Chakras 101

If you're interested in spiritual cleansing, you must know about your aura and chakras. Those who practice use their knowledge of these systems to send and receive healing energies, increase self-awareness, and manifest positive outcomes in life. This chapter explores these concepts' basics and how to manifest your highest potential. You will learn what they are, how you can sense and work with them, and the different ways to use them for personal growth. A better understanding of auras and chakras will unlock your body's potential energy to achieve your goals and fulfill your dreams. So, let's get started on your journey to unlocking your energy.

You need to gain a deeper understanding of your aura and chakras to achieve ultimate enlightenment

https://pixabay.com/es/illustrations/meditaci%c3%b3n-espiritual-yoga-zen-6988318/

Your Life Force

Energy has been a force flowing through every living being for centuries. It's essential for human existence, recognized as a vital component of physical and mental well-being. Many cultures have their names for this energy:

- *Qi* in Chinese medicine
- *Chi* in Japanese
- *Prana* in Ayurveda

Your energy, or qi, chi, or prana, is the force flowing throughout your body and supports your energetic existence. The chakras, the seven energy centers located throughout the body, are responsible for regulating energy flow. Each chakra is associated with a specific color, element, and body part. Each has unique properties associated with specific organs, feelings, and spiritual qualities.

The energy flowing through the chakras is often described as a river. It begins at the root chakra, at the base of the spine, and travels up through the other six chakras. Each chakra is like a dam, regulating energy circulation and ensuring it's distributed evenly throughout the body. When one chakra is blocked or not functioning correctly, it disrupts the energy flow and causes problems in other areas of the body.

Your Aura

Do you ever feel you can sense certain vibes or energy from other people? That's your aura. Your aura is the energy field surrounding the body and emanates from within. It's like a colorful halo giving insight into your emotional, physical, and spiritual state. Your aura is influenced by your chakras and vice versa. When chakras are balanced and open, your aura will be bright, vibrant, and full of positive energy. However, if your chakras are blocked or imbalanced, your aura appears dull, murky, or dark. Auras can be affected by external factors, like people and the environment.

An Overview of the Chakra System

Your aura and chakras are powerful and influential forces with the potential to shape you. They are part of the same energy system and work together, creating your overall energetic health.

- Your aura is the energy field surrounding and interpenetrating your physical body and comprises multiple energetic layers.
- Your chakras are the seven major energy centers within your aura corresponding to different physical, emotional, mental, and spiritual states of being.

How Your Aura and Chakras Connect

Your aura and chakras are closely connected and intertwined. Together, they act as a filter for the energy you take in from the outside world and the energy you expel into the world. Your aura is the energetic field surrounding your body and has distinct layers, each representing an aspect of your physical, mental, and spiritual being. These layers are connected to your seven chakras – energy centers and serve as gateways between your physical and spiritual realms. Your chakras and aura work together to keep your energy balanced and manifest your life's purpose. Your chakras' energy flows out through your aura to the external environment - the energy from the environment flows back in. When your chakras and aura are balanced, the energy flows freely, allowing positive energy, creativity, and spiritual growth. However, when your chakras and aura are out of balance, it can lead to physical, mental, and emotional blockages and negative energy. Understanding and working with your aura and chakras can increase your energy flow, balance your emotions, and create positive change in your life.

What Are Chakras?

The origin of chakras is a topic that has fascinated many people for centuries. They were developed to help people understand the complex relationship between the mind, body, and spirit. Over the years, the concept of chakras has spread beyond the borders of India. It has become a popular subject of study and practice in many parts of the world. Today, countless books, workshops, and classes are available dedicated to exploring the nature of chakras and their role in overall health and well-being.

Chakras are energy points in your body, specifically along the spine, strongly influencing your health and well-being. There are seven primary chakras:

- The Root Chakra (Muladhara)
- The Sacral Chakra (Svadhishthana)
- The Solar Plexus Chakra (Manipura)
- The Heart Chakra (Anahata)
- The Throat Chakra (Vishuddha)
- The Third Eye Chakra (Ajna)
- The Crown Chakra (Sahasrara)

Since each chakra is connected to life's physical, mental, emotional, and spiritual aspects, its vibration is associated with specific physical and spiritual attributes. They are the energy center of your body and the source of your spiritual power. You and your chakras are intrinsically linked. Each of the seven chakras is connected to a specific part of the body, a specific emotion, and the energies flowing through them. For example:

- The root chakra is related to the physical body.
- The heart chakra is related to the emotional body.
- The crown chakra is related to the spiritual body.

All your chakras are connected, forming a single, unified energy field; this is your aura. Your aura is more than just a colorful, ethereal energy field surrounding you. It's the sum of energy emitted by all your chakras combined. The chakras are the energy centers in your body that take in and transmit energy, from physical to emotional and then to spiritual. Each chakra has a specific purpose, and when you're out of balance, it is reflected in your aura. If one of your chakras is blocked, unbalanced, or overactive, it causes your aura to become stagnant or murky, leading to physical, mental, emotional, and spiritual issues.

On the other hand, when all your chakras are balanced, your aura radiates bright, vibrant energy. You can see from this that your chakras are directly related to your aura. If you want to maintain a healthy aura, you must take care of your chakras so that they can take in and transmit energy appropriately.

Why You Need to Learn about Your Chakras

Chakras are essential for spiritual awareness and development. Practitioners believe that by understanding and working with chakras, you can restore balance, heal, and reach higher states of consciousness.

All life force flows from the sacral chakra to the crown chakra, which simultaneously demands all seven to be open. When this happens, they align with the universe, providing greater insight and clarity. By understanding the chakras and their interaction, you'll better understand how your body and mind work together. With this knowledge, you become more aware of your inner self and feelings, more mindful of your physical and mental health, better decision-making, and live as your true self. In addition to physical and psychological health, the chakras help you become more spiritually conscious. You'll grow more in tune with your spiritual self as you work with them.

If you feel something is off or want to take the next step in your spiritual journey, you know where to look. Connecting with your chakras can open up a whole new world of possibilities and help you tap into the power within.

The Seven Chakras

The following comprehensive guide offers an in-depth exploration of the chakras, unveiling their hidden secrets and providing a clear road map to achieving and maintaining balance. Learn the scientific basis behind the chakras, their associated elements, and the spiritual significance of their location in the body.

The Root Chakra (Muladhara)

The root chakra.
Atarax42, CC0, via Wikimedia Commons https://commons.wikimedia.org/wiki/File:Chakra1.svg

The root chakra, or *Muladhara*, is the first energy center in the chakra system. It is a Sanskrit word meaning "root support" or "foundation." This chakra is located at the base of the spine, associated with red, and is the foundation of your energetic system. The root chakra is the energy center that essentially grounds you in your physical body and the physical world. Associated with the earth element, it is the source of your basic survival needs, responsible for your physical security, safety, and survival instincts. It's related to your sense of stability and foundation. You access your inner strength, courage, and determination from this energy center. The root chakra is the energy center of your physical body, which is why it is so important. When balanced and healthy, you feel safe, secure, and grounded in your physical form. As the foundation of your energetic system and the source of your inner strength and courage, it helps you access your inner power, strength, creativity, and passion. You might feel anxious, fearful, and overwhelmed when it is out of balance.

When your root chakra is open, you have access to the source of the physical world and your basic survival needs.

To open your root chakra, practitioners use meditation, yoga, and self-awareness. Additionally, thinking positively and practicing gratitude are helpful. A diet rich in vitamins, minerals, and proteins helps restore balance. Other methods like sound therapy and aromatherapy can open the root chakra.

The Sacral Chakra (Svadhishthana)

Sacral chakra.

Atarax42, CC0, via Wikimedia Commons https://commons.wikimedia.org/wiki/File:Chakra2.svg

The sacral chakra, or *Svadhishthana*, is located 2-3 inches below the navel at the lower end of the spine. This chakra is associated with orange and is the source of your creative and sexual energy. "Svadhishthana" is derived from the Sanskrit words "*svadhi*" (meaning "self") and "*sthana*" (meaning "place"). It is the center of your emotional being, governing your feelings, desires, and relationships. When this chakra is open, you experience the full range of feelings without fear. The sacral chakra is associated with the water element, more closely linked to your bodily fluids, and responsible for the energy flow between your physical body and your spiritual being.

Connected with pleasure and creativity, it is responsible for your desire and ability to experience healthy connections and intimacy. When the sacral chakra is open and balanced, you can fully express your feelings and desires and are free to explore and enjoy your sexuality. When the sacral chakra is blocked or out of balance, you experience various physical and psychological symptoms, including lower back pain, lethargy, lack of motivation, and difficulty expressing emotions and desires. Practitioners have reported feeling disconnected from their spiritual side and experiencing guilt, shame, or fear of their sexuality.

The sacral chakra is one of the most integral energy centers in the human body and is an integral part of your overall well-being. Engaging in activities allowing you to express your emotions and desires and fully enjoy your sexuality ensures this chakra is open and balanced. Activities include yoga, meditation, and creative pursuits like art and music. Practicing self-care is equally important, as you will nurture and connect with your spiritual side.

The Solar Plexus Chakra (Manipura)

Solar plexus chakra.
Atarax42, CC0, via Wikimedia Commons *https://commons.wikimedia.org/wiki/File:Chakra3.svg*

The solar plexus chakra, or *Manipura,* is an energy center in the abdominal region. This chakra is responsible for your personal power and is associated with yellow. The name Manipura is derived from Sanskrit, meaning "lustrous gem." The solar plexus chakra is located below your ribs, near the navel, where the three major energy channels, *ida, pingala,* and *sushumna,* meet. It is related to the digestive system and the endocrine glands, specifically the pancreas, adrenals, and liver. This chakra is associated with the element of fire and is the center of energy and dynamism. When the solar plexus chakra is balanced, you feel strong and self-confident. You can take the initiative and make decisions, be creative and brave, and have a strong sense of self-worth. Your purpose in life becomes clear, or you feel less stressed because of your good sense of direction.

When the solar plexus chakra is out of balance, you experience insecurity, fear, and low self-esteem. Powerlessness and lack of control overcome you, and some practitioners noted experiencing physical manifestations such as digestive problems, fatigue, and diabetes. Practice yoga and meditation, and focus on your breath to bring the solar plexus chakra back into balance. You can practice visualization and affirmations and focus on activities bringing joy and happiness. Crystals and gemstones like citrine,

yellow jade, and amber help bring this chakra back into balance. Finally, surround yourself with yellow to help remind you of your personal power.

The Heart Chakra (Anahata)

Heart chakra.
Atarax42, CC0, via Wikimedia Commons https://commons.wikimedia.org/wiki/File:Chakra4.svg

The heart chakra, or *Anahata*, is in the center of the chest and has a deep spiritual meaning and significance. The meaning of the word Anahata is "unhurt" or "unstuck," referring to the fact that this chakra is the center of love, compassion, and connection. The color associated with the heart chakra is green, symbolizing growth, harmony, and balance. The origin of the heart chakra comes from the subtleties of the body, the energy field related to all emotions and feelings. Its location is in the chest, just behind the sternum, at the same level as the heart. The heart chakra is associated with love, kindness, compassion, and acceptance and is the center of the higher self. It bridges the physical and spiritual realms and the connection between the conscious and subconscious minds.

When the heart chakra is open and balanced, you experience peace and harmony and become more open to receiving and giving love. The heart chakra is associated with trust, faith, and the ability to forgive. It is the gateway to higher consciousness and facilitates the connection to your divine nature. When it is open, you cultivate a deep connection to the divine and experience unconditional love in your life.

When the heart chakra is out of balance, you feel disconnected from your spiritual self and unable to feel joy and love. Practitioners observed the symptoms of an imbalanced heart chakra, including depression, anxiety, and disconnection from others. Meditation, yoga, and other mindfulness practices have proved useful in bringing balance to the heart chakra. Using crystals and essential oils helps open and balance the heart chakra.

Ultimately, the heart chakra is essential to your spiritual journey and supports self-awareness, love, kindness, and compassion for yourself and others. By balancing the heart chakra, you experience a deep spiritual connection and open yourself to experience unconditional love.

The Throat Chakra (Vishuddha)

Throat chakra.

Atarax42, CC0, via Wikimedia Commons *https://commons.wikimedia.org/wiki/File:Chakra5.svg*

The throat chakra, or *Vishuddha*, is located in the throat area. This chakra is associated with the element of Ether, and its color is blue. Vishuddha means "purification," reflecting its purpose in the body. The throat chakra is the fifth chakra and the bridge between the heart and the mind. It is the center of communication, expression, and creativity. When this chakra is blocked, it leads to insecurity, difficulty communicating, and a lack of creativity. The throat chakra is associated with the thyroid gland, the lungs, the vocal cords, the neck, and the jaw. When this chakra is balanced, it regulates metabolism and improves the functioning of the lungs. It encourages the healthy operation of the immune system and increases communication and creativity. The throat chakra is associated with true emotion. It promotes honesty and authenticity when balanced. To better understand your feelings, this chakra opens up the gateway to self-expression.

Practitioners noted that this chakra fosters purpose and a greater connection to the divine when fully opened. It helps improve relationships and generates inner peace and harmony.

The Third Eye Chakra (Ajna)

Third eye chakra.
Atarax42, CC0, via Wikimedia Commons https://commons.wikimedia.org/wiki/File:Chakra6.svg

The third eye chakra, or *Ajna*, is the sixth primary energy center of the body. It is located between the eyebrows, just above the bridge of the nose, and is represented by the color indigo. This chakra is associated with psychic ability and is often called the "*mind's eye.*" The origin of the third eye chakra dates back to ancient India, where it was believed to be the seat of wisdom and intuition. In yoga, the third eye chakra is the first to open, allowing access to the higher realms of consciousness. As the third eye chakra is activated, it develops intuition and the ability to perceive the spiritual realm. The third eye chakra is associated with the element of light, developed through meditation. Working with this chakra helps to open your mind, allowing you to tap into your inner wisdom. It is associated with the pineal gland, which regulates the hormones governing your feelings, sleep, and stress.

When the third eye chakra is balanced, it reduces fear and anxiety and increases peace and contentment. It is associated with the pine cone, symbolizing the gateway to the higher realms of consciousness. When it is open and balanced, you have more access to your inner wisdom and insight into the deeper mysteries of life.

The Crown Chakra (Sahasrara)

Crown chakra.
https://pixabay.com/es/illustrations/corona-chakra-energ%c3%ada-chi-2533113/

The crown chakra, or *Sahasrara,* is the highest of the chakras and the most divine. It is the source of spiritual energy and is the primary center for enlightenment and divine wisdom. The crown chakra is associated with violet and white and is located at the top of the head. The origin of Sahasrara comes from the ancient Hindu practice of Kundalini yoga. The crown chakra is activated during this practice, opening the gateway to spiritual consciousness and divine connection. It is often called the "thousand-petaled lotus" or "thousand-spoked wheel." The crown chakra is about connecting with the divine and transcending the physical realm. It is associated with spiritual awakening, enlightenment, self-realization, and ultimate spiritual transformation. When open, practitioners report a higher consciousness and are the source of divine wisdom, cosmic knowledge, and consciousness.

The human body is complex and fascinating. You can go beyond the physical form and explore the energy radiating around you. That energy is your aura and is affected by your thoughts, emotions, and other influences. You can strengthen and balance your aura through the chakras. Chakras are energy centers correlating to different areas of the body. You can experience physical, mental, and emotional symptoms when they are out of balance. By working with your chakras, you can balance and harmonize your energy and create a stronger, healthier aura. Essentially, your aura and chakras are an integral part of your being, and taking the time to nurture and nourish them creates a strong and vibrant energy field.

Chapter 3: Cleansing Your Aura and Chakras

Cleansing your aura and chakras is an essential practice for keeping your energy level high and your mind clear. This spiritual tradition offers a way to balance your body, mind, and spirit. It involves cleansing your energy field of obstructions, negativity, or stagnant energy and restoring it to its natural, vibrant state. You achieve a greater sense of balance, clarity, and peace through meditation, visualization, and other techniques. This chapter explores how you can increase your energy, improve your mental and emotional well-being, and manifest your desires more easily through regular cleansing of your aura and chakras. Whether seeking to deepen your spiritual practice or wanting to stay centered in a chaotic world, cleansing your aura and chakras is a great way to start.

Meditation and visualization will help you reach a higher state of mind.
https://unsplash.com/photos/V-TIPBoC_2M

Cleansing Your Seven Chakras

Your aura is the energy center of your body, and it must be cleansed regularly to avoid blockage in the energy flow. Regular cleansing of your chakras helps remove negative energy and stress from your body, leaving your aura full of positivity and joy. It improves your mental and physical health and eliminates the impurities from your energy field, making it more vibrant and powerful. Cleansing your aura and chakras will build self-confidence and self-awareness as it clarifies your thoughts and feelings. Moreover, it balances your feelings, helping you to stay focused and connected with your inner being. The following methods for each chakra will keep your energy balanced and in harmony with the universe.

The Root Chakra (Muladhara)

Have you ever felt stuck in a rut? Like, no matter what you do, you can't seem to move forward? It could signify that your root chakra is blocked. This chakra is the foundation of your energy system and governs your sense of security and stability. When blocked, it feels like the ground has been pulled out from under you. You feel disconnected from your sense of belonging, safety, and sometimes your body. It leads to anxiety, fear, panic, and depression. Physically, you may experience lower back pain, digestive issues, and a general imbalance. Unblocking your root chakra is a major step toward balance and harmony in your life. You will feel:

- A newfound confidence and stability
- More grounded, centered in your body, and less easily swayed by external forces
- More connected to your physical environment, with a deeper appreciation for the natural world's beauty and abundance
- Improved digestion, elimination, and overall vitality
- More energized and less prone to fatigue
- Chronic health issues resolve themselves

Fortunately, various techniques are available to cleanse and unblock your root chakra. The first step is to know the source of the blockages and practice mindfulness to understand where your energy is blocked. Visualization is a powerful tool. Imagine a red light radiating from the base of your spine. Visualize this energy moving up and out of your body. Feel the energy vibrating and activating all the cells in your body.

Other techniques include:

- Using affirmations. Repeat positive statements such as, "I am safe and secure" and "I am connected to my source of power."

- Practice yoga postures specifically designed to open the root chakra, such as child's pose and mountain pose.

- Spend time in nature, as being in the presence of the elements helps connect you to the Earth's energy.

- Listening to calming music, meditating, and spending time with loved ones are beneficial.

The Sacral Chakra (Svadhishthana)

The sacral chakra is responsible for your creativity, feelings, and sexuality. When this chakra is blocked, it can lead to disconnection from the physical and emotional realms. It manifests in numerous ways, from feeling emotionally blocked and unable to express yourself to feeling stuck in an unfulfilling job or relationship. When you have a blocked sacral chakra, you feel like you're being held back, with no outlet for your creative energy and passions. You may experience fear of change, low self-esteem, and shame and guilt. Physically, you may feel lethargic, drained of energy, and have difficulty focusing. You may even experience physical symptoms such as digestive issues and a lack of sexual desire. How does it feel when you unblock this powerful energy center? You'll notice:

- Inspiration flows effortlessly through you

- Ideas and solutions to problems that were once insurmountable suddenly become clear and accessible

- A heightened pleasure and sensuality

- A greater appreciation for the world's beauty around you

- A newfound ability to fully enjoy life's simple pleasures

But, perhaps the most profound effect of unblocking your sacral chakra is deep emotional healing. Old wounds and traumas buried for years can finally surface, allowing you to confront and process them healthily. It leads to greater self-awareness and a more authentic connection to your true self.

You can use various techniques to cleanse and unblock your sacral chakra and restore your balance. Firstly, you can use meditation to access the energy of your sacral chakra.

1. Sit comfortably, close your eyes, and focus on your breath. Imagine a bright orange light entering your body just below the navel. Spend a few minutes visualizing the light entering and surrounding your sacral chakra. This will open and activate your sacral chakra's energy, allowing it to flow freely.

2. Use crystals, specifically orange stones like carnelian, coral, and orange calcite. Place the stone on your lower abdomen and lie down for a few minutes. Visualize the crystal's energy entering your sacral chakra, unlocking it, and restoring balance.

3. Practice yoga asanas, like the Half-Bound Lotus pose and Hip Openers.

4. Eat a healthy and balanced diet. Eating foods rich in vitamins and minerals, like fruit, vegetables, and nuts, will nourish your body and help restore your aura.

The Solar Plexus Chakra (Manipura)

When your solar plexus is blocked, it can be uncomfortable. This chakra is located between the navel and the diaphragm and is the third chakra of the body. When it is blocked, you feel a lack of direction or power or feel stuck. You feel anxious, overwhelmed, and powerless, as if you cannot take control of your life. You experience physical symptoms such as indigestion, headaches, or fatigue. You experience low self-esteem and insecurity. When the solar plexus chakra is blocked, it can be difficult to move forward in life. You may be unable to break free because you constantly struggle with self-doubt and lack of confidence, making deciding or taking action difficult. But when you unblock your solar plexus chakra, it's like a burst of sunshine in your life.

- You feel empowered, confident, and ready to take on the world

- You no longer second-guess yourself or doubt your abilities

- You trust your intuition and have a clear purpose

- Physically, you notice increased energy and better digestion

- Emotionally, you are more in control of your thoughts and feelings

- You no longer let external factors dictate your mood or outlook on life

- You have inner peace and contentment

Affirmations are one of the most effective ways to unblock your solar plexus chakra. Positive affirmations increase your self-confidence and encourage you to take action to achieve your goals.

Other techniques include:

- Practicing mindful meditation. It focuses your attention on the present moment and emotional state to bring you clarity and reduce stress and anxiety.

- Breathwork. Take time to sit in a comfortable position and take slow, deep breaths. It raises awareness of the solar plexus chakra area in the diaphragm. You will become more relaxed and aware of your physical and emotional state.

- Practicing yoga. Many yoga poses, such as the Boat Pose, the Sun Salutation, and the Warrior I, can open this chakra.

The Heart Chakra (Anahata)

When your heart chakra is blocked, it can lead to a wide range of physical, emotional, and spiritual issues. Physically, a blocked heart chakra can manifest as chest pain, difficulty breathing, poor circulation, and heart palpitations. Emotionally, it can lead to loneliness, isolation, lack of empathy and joy, and depression. Spiritually, it can lead to a feeling of disconnection from the world, not feeling part of something larger than yourself, and a lack of purpose.

What does it feel like when your heart chakra is blocked? Generally, it feels like your heart is being squeezed – like you're disconnected from your emotions, don't have the energy to reach out to others, and are stuck in despair. It makes it difficult to experience joy, contentment, and connection to the world around you. Fortunately, you can use various techniques to cleanse your heart chakra and balance your life.

- **Practice self-love.** You need to recognize and appreciate your self-worth to unblock your heart chakra. Spend time with yourself, practice self-care, and remind yourself of your positive qualities. It will help you open up to love and connection with others.

- **Practice yoga and meditation.** These activities have the power to open and balance your energy centers, including the heart chakra. Focusing on your breath, repeating mantras, and practicing yoga postures clarifies and balances your life.

- **Surround yourself with positive energy.** Spend time with friends and family who make you feel uplifted and connected. Distance yourself from negative people and situations, and make time to relax and nurture your spirit.

- **Permit yourself to feel.** Recognize and accept your feelings, no matter how uncomfortable they are. Allow yourself to express how you feel, and don't be afraid to speak the truth, even to yourself.

The Throat Chakra (Vishuddha)

When your throat chakra is blocked, it can be a difficult and uncomfortable experience. The throat chakra is associated with communication and self-expression, so it's hard to find the words to express yourself when it is blocked. A blocked throat chakra is described as a lump in the throat or tightness in the chest as if something is stopping you from speaking. You may feel you cannot truly express yourself or are being silenced. You could experience physical symptoms such as a sore throat, hoarseness, difficulty swallowing, and neck and shoulder tension. Emotionally, you could feel frustrated, fearful, and anxious and have difficulty speaking up for yourself or expressing your needs. All these feelings and physical symptoms are signs that your throat chakra is blocked and needs attention. But what happens when you finally free it? It feels like a breath of fresh air.

- You feel a release as if a weight has been lifted off your shoulders.

- Expressing yourself authentically, without fear of judgment or rejection, is easier.

- Words flow effortlessly, so you become more confident in communicating effectively.

- Physically, you feel lightness in your throat area, as if the tension has been released.

- You notice an improvement in your overall health, as the throat chakra is connected to the thyroid gland and immune system.

There are various techniques for cleansing your throat chakra.

- One of the most popular methods is to practice chanting "OM," a vibration to cleanse and open the throat chakra. Chants like mantras "OM Shanti OM" or "OM Namah

Shivaya" also work wonders for opening the energy channels in the throat.

- Another technique is to practice yoga asanas specifically targeting the throat chakra, including poses like the Shoulder stand, Plow, Fish, and Cobra. These poses help open up the throat's energy and allow better communication.

- You can practice visualization to free your throat chakra. Visualize a blue light radiating from your throat and connecting you with the divine. As the light shines brighter, feel the tension in the area melt away.

- Finally, practice deep breathing. It relaxes the throat muscles and encourages the energy to flow freely. Take deep, calming breaths and focus on the energy in your throat.

The Third Eye Chakra (Ajna)

When your third eye chakra is blocked, it feels like you are living life on autopilot and lacking purpose. When things get rough, you become aware you're stuck in the same patterns, unable to break free. When you can't see the bigger picture, you blame yourself because you cannot trust your intuition which helps you to see it clearly. You may find it hard to focus and concentrate and have difficulty making decisions or finding clarity. Interpreting and understanding your feelings and those of others is difficult. You feel disconnected from your intuition and spiritual guidance. You may struggle with restlessness and anxiety, depression, confusion, and a lack of inspiration. These are signs that your third eye chakra is blocked. But when you free your third eye chakra, the real magic happens in your perception. Suddenly, you see things differently.

- Colors appear brighter
- Shapes are more defined
- You experience heightened intuition, as if you can sense things beyond the physical realm

It's not uncommon to feel a sense of awe and wonder at this newfound perception as you connect to something greater than yourself. It's a truly profound experience that can change how you see the world.

The good news? There are various techniques for cleansing and unblocking it to connect more with your higher self.

- One of the most common ways to free your third eye chakra is through meditation. Focusing your attention on your third eye and repeating affirmations like "I trust my intuition" can break through blocks and open your third eye chakra.

- Visualization is another great way to cleanse and unblock this chakra. Visualize a white light coming in and opening your third eye, allowing your intuition to flow freely.

- Crystals, specifically amethyst, sodalite, and lapis lazuli, create alignment and balance by interacting with the body's aura. Place the crystal over your third eye or hold it while meditating to free it.

- Yoga is an excellent method. Poses like the Bridge and the Plow enhance the body's energy flow. As you move through these poses, focus on your third eye and visualize it opening.

- Finally, using essential oils like lavender and jasmine aromatherapy will open and balance your third eye chakra. You can diffuse the oils in your home or use them in an aromatherapy massage.

The Crown Chakra (Sahasrara)

When your crown chakra, the highest of the seven chakras, is blocked, it can create a disconnection from yourself and the world around you. You might feel stuck in a state of anxiety, depression, or confusion. It manifests in physical symptoms, such as headaches, fatigue, and poor concentration. It can lead to spiritual issues, like a lack of motivation or an inability to focus on spiritual matters - perhaps you're constantly questioning your life's purpose and feel disconnected from your true self. It can be a difficult and disorienting experience, like living in a fog and being unable to connect with the real you. You may feel trapped in your mind and unable to move forward with your life. If your crown chakra is blocked, you must take steps to free it to experience joy, peace, and connection. Unblocking your crown chakra is a life-changing experience. It's like removing a veil covering your eyes, preventing you from seeing life's beauty and magic.

- You're more connected to your higher self
- Intuition is easier to access

- You're more aware of the synchronicities and signs the universe is sending you

- You feel more grounded and centered

- You can navigate life better

Luckily, there are various techniques for cleansing your crown chakra and restoring balance to your life.

- One of the best ways is through meditation. By sitting quietly and focusing on your breath, you can tap into the energy of this chakra, refocus and restore balance. During your meditation, imagine a white or golden light radiating from the top of your head.

- Certain yoga poses can open the crown chakra and balance the body and mind. Use poses like the Lotus, Padmasana, Corpse Pose, or Savasana for peace and harmony.

- Aromatherapy using essential oils like jasmine, frankincense, and rose can create calmness and serenity. Add a few drops of your chosen oil to a diffuser and breathe in the aroma throughout the day.

- Clear quartz, amethyst, and selenite are all excellent crystals for this chakra. Place one or more of these crystals on the crown of your head while you meditate or rest.

As an extra tip, eat foods associated with each color and element of the chakra you want to free to help you cleanse and balance your chakras. For example, root vegetables like carrots and beets can help with the root chakra, while fruit like oranges and pineapples can help with the sacral chakra.

How to Meditate and Visualize

Meditation and visualization are the two most popular techniques for unblocking your chakras. Here are some tips for these methods.

Basic Meditation

To begin your meditation practice, find a comfortable place where you can sit or lie down, preferably with no distractions. Close your eyes and focus on your breathing. Take deep breaths, inhaling through your nostrils and exhaling slowly. Allow your thoughts to come and go without judgment. Keep your mind in the present moment and be conscious of your thoughts without reacting. Visualize yourself in a state of peace and tranquility and let go of negative or anxious thoughts.

Focus on each chakra, one at a time. Visualize each chakra's color, element, purpose, and location as you focus on the sensations you experience. Meditation can be done for as little as five minutes a day or as long as you like. As you practice more often, it will be easier to reach a state of complete meditation and reap the benefits.

Basic Visualization

Visualization is a powerful technique for freeing chakras and allowing energy to flow freely. To begin visualizing, find a comfortable spot and settle. Take a few deep breaths, inhaling and exhaling slowly. As you breathe, focus on the area that needs healing and envision a bright, golden light entering this area and filling it with warmth and healing energy. Visualize the chakras opening up, allowing the prana to flow. For example, picture the energy flowing through the body like a river, or envision different colors radiating from the chakras. Visualization is a powerful tool for freeing chakras, and with practice and patience, it can profoundly change your energy field.

Aura and chakras are your body's energy centers and must be cleansed regularly to avoid obstructions in the energy flow. If you've felt a shift in the room without an explanation or had a negative thought creep up and linger in your mind for days, your aura and chakras could need cleansing. Cleansing is an ancient practice used for thousands of years by practitioners to feel more grounded, balanced, and connected to the universe. It is a simple yet powerful technique to restore your natural energy and amplify your spiritual well-being.

Regular cleansing focuses on the area of each chakra with a specific technique. Cleansing opens the door to clarity, creativity, and higher consciousness when done correctly. Cleansing your chakras is an essential part of spiritual practice and a powerful tool for improving overall health and well-being.

Chapter 4: Meditation to Raise Your Vibration

Meditation is a powerful tool to help you raise your vibration, create positive energy, and find inner peace. When your vibration is raised to a higher frequency, it naturally attracts more positive experiences. Your thoughts' vibrations impact how you experience life in many ways. With meditation, you can learn to control and raise your thoughts and intentions' vibrations to manifest positive results in all areas of life with meditation.

Vibrational frequency plays a pivotal role in your journey to enlightenment.
https://unsplash.com/photos/VsI_74zRzAo

This chapter explores the concept of vibrational frequency and how it relates to meditation. It discusses the basics of this simple yet profound practice. It provides a step-by-step guide to meditating to raise your vibration and explains how to make the most of this experience, including tips on modifying the meditation for busy readers who may not always have the time or patience for a long session.

What Is Vibrational Frequency: How Can It Help

Vibrational frequency is the concept of energy flowing through and around the body at all times. All living things emit a particular vibration, either positive or negative.

Low vibrational frequencies are associated with negative emotions like sadness, anger, and fear. The more negative thoughts and emotions experienced, the lower the vibration. On the other hand, high vibrational frequencies are associated with positive emotions like joy, love, and gratitude. The vibrations rise when you open your heart and mind to love and positivity.

Raising your vibration increases your energy and frequency to attract more positive experiences. It is achieved by changing your thoughts and feelings about yourself and the world around you. Transformation happens when your thoughts shift from negative to positive, creating a higher vibrational state.

The Benefits of Raising Your Vibration

One of the most powerful practices is raising your vibration when improving your overall well-being and finding true fulfillment. You can transform many aspects of your life by boosting your energetic frequency. Here are some of the most profound benefits you can experience when raising your vibration:

Improved Mental and Emotional Well-being

You can experience heightened mental and emotional well-being by raising your vibrational frequency. As your vibration rises, the negative energy you have been carrying dissipates and is replaced with peace and contentment. Staying grounded in positive thoughts and emotions is much easier, and you will become less prone to depression or anxiety.

Clarity and Focus

When the vibration is raised, you can access higher awareness and understanding. You become more in tune with yourself, the world around you, and how you fit into it. Many people struggle with scattered thoughts or are overwhelmed, but when you raise your energetic frequency, you develop a sharper mental focus and better understand the path ahead. This heightened consciousness can lead to greater self-awareness and clarity.

Healthier Connections

The higher the vibrational frequency, the healthier and more meaningful your connections with others become. When you increase your energetic vibration, it's much easier to attract like-minded people on the same level as you are emotionally and spiritually. Your friends and family can help you to stay on track manifesting the life of your dreams.

You can give and receive love more freely, creating a solid foundation to express yourself honestly. With each connection you make, your confidence will grow as you find joy in being part of something greater than yourself.

Increased Abundance

The more you raise your vibration, the more abundance you can experience. It's like a ripple effect – the higher your vibration, the more space you create for increased quantity to enter. Abundance comes in many forms; financial resources, opportunities, relationships, and health.

Changing your mindset and focusing on what you want instead of what you don't have opens up more possibilities and attracts abundance.

The Effects of Low Vibration

Low vibration energies can have the opposite effect. This energy is associated with negativity, stagnation, and unhappiness. It hinders the ability to create positive experiences for you and those around you. The lower the vibrational frequency, the less likely it is that you will attract what you want.

Low-vibration feelings can lead to unhealthy life patterns. You may get stuck in cycles of negative thinking, and it becomes harder to break free from them. Without raising your vibration to a higher frequency, you will more likely experience fear, anger, or helplessness and be consumed by these emotions.

Although low-vibration energy seems overwhelming, there are ways to raise your vibration and experience its positive effects. You can learn how to shift your frequency and become a powerful manifesto of all good things with practice.

How Meditating and Raising Your Vibration Can Change Your Life

The best way to raise your vibration is through meditation. Through regular meditation practice, you increase the energy frequency and become more consciously aware of thoughts and feelings. This heightened awareness helps develop authentic connections, and meditation allows you to become more open and accepting of life's changes. Here is a simple yet effective meditation exercise to raise your vibration:

1. Start by Grounding Yourself

Grounding yourself is an essential first step in meditation practice. Grounding helps reduce stress and anxiety and also helps you to feel more connected to your body and the physical world around you. By grounding yourself, you can better tap into the energy of your higher vibrations and focus on what matters most.

Sit or lie on the floor and consciously connect with your breath. Take deep breaths and focus on feeling safely grounded and connected to the Earth, like being rooted like a tree or standing firmly on solid ground. This will help you feel more present and related to the energy around you. Take a few moments to feel grounded before moving on to the next step.

2. Practice Breathing Exercises to Raise Your Vibration

Inhale deeply through your nose and exhale slowly through your mouth. As you breathe in, imagine the energy from the universe entering and filling all your cells with light. As you exhale, visualize negative energy leaving your body and returning to its source. Repeat this breathwork for several minutes, focusing on your breath and feeling filled with light energy.

3. Posing Techniques to Increase Your Frequency

Next, take a few moments to move into various poses to help raise your vibration even further. Stand comfortably with your feet firmly planted on the ground. Take a few deep breaths, focus on opening your heart, and let go of negative or blocked energy. Then, slowly raise your arms above your head in a V-shape and take another deep breath, imagining all the universe's frequencies entering your fingertips as you reach the sky. Continue to explore various poses to open up your body, release negativity, and allow the energies around you to fill you.

4. Incorporate Visualization Techniques to Stay Centered

While in these poses, imagine yourself surrounded by an orb of white light for a few moments. This light is filled with healing energy and protection from negative frequencies. Imagine being energized by this light and feeling more connected to your highest self. Visualize radiating with light and energy and feeling more open, expansive, and connected; let the light fill you and cleanse your energy.

Meditating on the Go: Tips for Busy People

Meditation can be a challenging activity to maintain, especially when you lead a hectic lifestyle. Fortunately, with a few creative strategies, it is possible to cultivate and embody mindfulness even in your busiest moments.

Set Aside 10 Minutes a Day

Dedicate 10-15 minutes of your day to meditation. Even if it's only 10 minutes, it can help you to stay focused and connected to yourself and the energies around you. You don't need much time for meditation; even a few minutes can make a difference in your day.

When you start, don't put too much pressure on yourself. Start small and increase the time when it feels comfortable to do so. Set your phone's alarm to remind you to take 10 minutes for a mini meditation session.

Use Guided Meditations

If you don't have the time or energy to sit down and practice traditional meditation, try guided meditation. Plenty of free and paid audio recordings can help you to relax and re-center yourself. Start with a simple breathing exercise and gradually move on to different guided meditations as you become more comfortable.

Look for an app to help make meditation more accessible, like those designed specifically for people with busy lives. You can use these apps to guide and remind you when and where to practice mindfulness for a short period, whether for 5 minutes or an hour.

Take Advantage of Small Pockets of Time

Taking short breaks throughout the day gives you time to reset your mind and re-energize your body. These moments are essential for cultivating mindfulness but don't require dedicated chunks of time exclusively for meditation practice.

While waiting in line, on public transportation, or taking a lunch break, become aware of your breath and observe sensations arising within your body without judgment or attachment.

Practice Mindful Breathing

If you can't get away from work during the day, practice mindful breathing wherever you are, at your desk, or walking down the street if necessary. All it takes is five minutes to focus on your breath movement and relax into stillness before returning to your task.

Allow yourself this small gesture of compassion. Permit yourself to step out and practice self-reflection whenever needed. It could be as simple as taking one deep breath before beginning a difficult task or project during work hours.

Get Creative with Your Practice

There are many ways to incorporate meditation without sitting still for long periods. Walking or running is a form of moving meditation. Focus on the present moment and be mindful during your daily tasks. For example, folding laundry can become a mindful task if you pay attention to the feeling of the fabric in your hands and focus on each article as you fold it.

Use Your Morning and Evening Commutes

Your morning commute might not seem like the ideal place for meditation, but with the right attitude, it can be done. If traveling by public transport, use this time instead of checking emails or scrolling through social media. Harness this period by training your attention on something more productive, like conscious breathing while staring out the window.

Listen to relaxing music to help clear your mind clutter and tune inwards rather than being distracted by what's happening around you. Prepare mentally for what lies ahead at work or home after returning from the commute.

Bring Meditation Practices into Your Everyday Activities

Meditation can be something other than a dedicated practice. You can bring mindfulness into your everyday activities, such as washing dishes, gardening, or taking a shower, by focusing on the present moment and being aware of what is happening around you. It helps with relaxation and creating peace within yourself.

You can practice mindful eating, an exceptionally great habit to form when trying to stay focused on healthy habits. Before eating, take a moment to notice the food in front of you - its color, aroma, texture, etc. You will appreciate the food and savor every bite rather than mindlessly snacking.

Incorporate Walking Meditations into Your Daily Routine

Walking meditations are a great way to become more aware and present in your body. They can be done indoors or outdoors and focus on each step and sensations arising in the body during the process.

Start by taking slow and deliberate steps with mindful awareness of each footfall. As you walk, note the surrounding scenery and sounds and allow your senses to be fully engaged. You can add breathing exercises into the routine by focusing on the breath's rhythm as you walk.

Stay Consistent

Consistency is the key to making a practice a regular part of your life. Set a reminder every day to take time out for yourself and meditate. The more consistent you are with your practice, the easier it will become.

Remember, meditation is not about achieving perfection but connecting to yourself in the moment. The more you practice, the more mindful moments you can incorporate into your everyday life.

More Ways to Raise Your Vibration

The practice of meditation is an essential tool to raise your vibration to become more present and connected. There are many ways to raise your vibration.

Get Out in Nature: Nature has unique ways of lifting your spirits and raising your vibration. Taking the time to get out in nature, whether a simple walk in the park or an extended hike in the mountains, can be incredibly therapeutic for the body and mind. When you are outside, surrounded by trees, animals, plants, and fresh air, you reconnect with yourself and recharge your energy.

Plan Small Vacations: Nothing can raise your vibration like a vacation when you feel bogged down by the daily grind. Taking yourself away from the hustle and bustle of everyday life allows more time to rest, relax, and be present in the moment.

Short vacations are a great way to break away from your everyday routines and raise your vibration. Whether a weekend trip to the countryside or a week-long stay in another country, these breaks give you space and time to enjoy yourself, relax, and enjoy the little things life offers.

Listen to Calming Music: When listening to music, you can access deep relaxation and energy. Calming music, like classical pieces or nature sounds, can help shift mood and raise your vibration instantly. Spending time with music is an opportunity for self-reflection and greater self-understanding.

Eat Healthy, Nourishing Foods: What you put into your body directly affects vibration and energy levels. Eating healthy, nutritious foods reduces stress and fatigue, leaving you feeling more energized and positive. A healthy diet full of fresh fruit, vegetables, superfoods, nuts, and seeds can help to restore balance to the body and mind.

Other healthy eating habits to include in your diet are avoiding processed and sugary foods, meal prepping, eating mindfully, and drinking plenty of water throughout the day.

Practicing Forgiveness and Mindfulness: Forgiveness is critical to raising positive vibration and letting go of negative energy. Practicing forgiveness can be difficult, but it is essential for releasing resentment or hurt you're holding onto. It can help heal relationships and bridge divides that have been created. Mindfulness is being present and aware in each moment without judgment. Practicing mindfulness helps you stay connected to yourself and the world around you instead of retreating into your thoughts or worries. It enhances the ability to experience joy and peace and be present for others.

Connecting with Kindness, Gratitude, and Abundance: Focusing on being kind to yourself and others helps raise vibration and energy levels. The same goes for cultivating gratitude and abundance. When expressing gratitude for small, everyday blessings, you can shift perception to appreciation and contentment. Focusing on the abundance already in your life helps you recognize the wealth of available resources. It opens new possibilities and opportunities and helps you lead a more meaningful life.

Engage in Activities that Bring Joy: Joy raises the vibration and is essential for a balanced life. Activities that bring joy, like dancing or playing a sport, can keep you connected with life. Remember, pleasure doesn't have to be big or grandiose; it can come in something as simple as making time for yourself every day.

Surround Yourself with Positive People: Surrounding yourself with positive people helps raise your vibration and increases self-confidence. When surrounded by those who support, encourage, and bring out the best in you, you feel more connected and fulfilled. Through shared experiences and conversations, you can learn from one another, challenge yourself and become the best version of yourself. Choose those who lift you up instead of bringing you down when selecting your inner circle.

Meditation is an incredibly powerful tool for tapping into your highest vibration. Meditating connects you with yourself deeper and accesses your inner wisdom. You can use meditation to clear negative energy or self-limiting beliefs holding you back so that you can move forward in life with greater clarity and purpose. Meditation helps restore balance and peace in the body, releasing tension or stress. Remember, raising your vibration is an ongoing practice; it requires dedication, commitment, and consistency to see lasting results. With patience and perseverance, you can reap the rewards of higher vibration, mentally and physically. So, take time today and tap into your highest vibration.

Chapter 5: The Healing Power of Reiki

Are you feeling stressed, uncertain, and not quite sure of how to make sense of the world we live in today? The Healing Power of Reiki may be just what you need. Many people have heard of it but don't understand how it works or why it's so powerful.

Reiki is an ancient healing practice that originated in Japan over 2000 years ago. It is based on the concept of "ki" or "chi," which is a life force energy existing in all living beings and connecting to the universe. Reiki channels this energy throughout the body to help it heal naturally. "Reiki" comes from two Japanese words, "rei," meaning universal, and "ki," meaning energy, translated as "universal life energy." It is based on the belief that all living things have an energy field or life force that must be balanced and harmonized for physical and emotional well-being. Reiki practitioners use their hands to channel positive energy into a person's body to promote relaxation and healing.

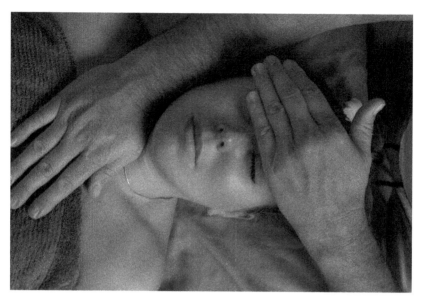
Reiki is an ancient healing practice that will allow you to cleanse your spirit.
https://www.pexels.com/photo/close-up-shot-of-a-woman-having-a-massage-5573584/

Reiki can be used as a preventative wellness measure and curative medicine - helping people with physical pain or emotional distress find relief without relying solely on medications or invasive treatments with unwanted side effects. It has benefited people with chronic conditions like fibromyalgia, arthritis, and mental health issues, like depression and anxiety, by helping them find greater balance within themselves while relieving their symptoms. Reiki can help increase the clarity of thought and aid better decision-making skills due to its ability to open up blocked energetic pathways inhibiting the ability to think clearly and make rational life decisions.

Origins

Reiki was first developed by a Japanese Buddhist monk, Mikao Usui, in 1922 after he experienced a spiritual awakening while meditating on Mount Kurama. During his time on the mountain, Usui felt a deep connection to ki's healing power and discovered how to use it for healing purposes. He spent several years studying and experimenting with this powerful form of healing before finally founding the Usui System of Reiki Healing.

Usui developed a system of five principles that form the basis of Reiki today. They are just for today, don't get angry, don't worry, be grateful, and do your best. In addition to these principles, three levels of Reiki practice require attunement by a teacher: Shoden (beginner level), Okuden (intermediate level), and Shinpiden (master level). Before moving on to the next level, the practitioner must demonstrate proficiency in each precedent level.

Since then, Reiki has continued to evolve and was brought to the Western world in the late 19th century by Dr. Chujiro Hayashi, who studied under Usui's teachings. In 1937, he opened his clinic, offering treatments to many people worldwide. In 1938, he introduced Reiki classes at universities so others could learn these techniques.

Today, Reiki is practiced worldwide by millions of people who believe using this technique helps them reach better mental, physical, and emotional balance. Practitioners use various hand positions above or on their client's bodies, focusing on their breath and allowing natural energy to flow freely through them while connecting deeply with their clients. During this process, they create an atmosphere filled with love and acceptance, allowing for deep healing within you and between humans who share this experience.

How Does Reiki Work?

Reiki balances the body's natural energies at its core through various hand placements called mudras. When these mudras are used correctly during a Reiki session, it helps restore the balance between the mind and body and enhance your overall well-being. During a typical session, practitioners use a light touch to direct positive energy into areas of the body that need it most - such as tension points or areas affected by illness or injury – while calming affirmations help release negative energy. Depending on individual needs, a session typically lasts 30 minutes to an hour.

Reiki practitioners believe illness can be caused by blocked energy pathways in the body. Using their hands to transfer life force energy into their client's bodies (channeled energy), they restore harmony within their client's systems and help them regain balance and wellness. The practitioner does not heal but instead channels the life force energy so that it can work on its recipient's behalf.

The practice consists of two main components:

1. **Hand placements** (or hand positions) on specific areas of the body corresponding with different parts of the body's energetic

pathways.

2. **Intention setting** – this includes visualizing white light entering through your hands into your client's body while thinking positive thoughts for their well-being. Through these two aspects, practitioners can create an environment for healing and restoration within their client's bodies.

One example of Reiki healing is pain relief. When a person's muscles are tense due to physical or emotional stress, Reiki helps them relax by balancing the energies in their body's pathways. Reiki helps reduce inflammation, easing pain and discomfort associated with muscle tension and stiffness caused by injuries or illnesses, such as chronic fatigue syndrome or fibromyalgia. Many people report feeling energized after sessions because Reiki helps promote circulation throughout the body, providing beneficial nutrients while removing toxins deeper than most conventional treatments can reach.

Another example is helping people with anxiety disorders. Since Reiki works on physical and emotional levels, it can be extremely helpful for those with anxiety or depression. It helps restore balance throughout their mind, body, and spirit, promoting peace and relaxation instead of fear and worry. The client can move through difficult times more easily than if they were dealing with those emotions alone without help from outside sources like Reiki therapy sessions. In addition, many people find it helpful in treating sleep disorders. One common side effect is feeling relaxed enough so the client drifts into deep sleep quicker than normal after receiving a Reiki treatment. Practicing regularly with other healthy lifestyle choices like proper nutrition and exercise allows them to get better rest, positively impacting all other aspects of their life, including mental, emotional, physical, and spiritual wellbeing.

Reiki has been especially effective at helping stroke victims recover faster. Research studies have shown that clients who received regular Reiki treatments showed improved motor skills within weeks compared to those who did not receive this therapy combined with traditional medical interventions like occupational and physical therapies. It suggests that due to its ability to reduce inflammation and increase circulation throughout the body's systems, Reiki can speed up recovery times in certain cases.

Reiki has many benefits, including:

- Reducing stress and anxiety
- Promoting relaxation
- Improving sleep quality
- Increasing immunity boosts circulation
- Aiding muscle recovery
- Relieving pain and headaches
- Speeding up recovery times
- Providing clarity and insight into life paths

It's clear why so many people globally are turning toward this traditional healing modality nowadays rather than solely relying on Western medicine.

The 5 Reiki Principles

1. "Just for today, I will not be angry."

The first Reiki principle is "Just for today; I will not be angry." This notion emphasizes the importance of letting go of negative emotions and allowing yourself to live in the present moment. When you step back and observe your current situation, you can better understand how anger does not help you. Instead, it creates further tension by blocking energy flow and depriving you of thinking clearly.

When practicing this principle, you become aware of your thoughts and emotions before they cause harm. You become mindful of feelings and consider how each decision could potentially affect others. By taking a step back and looking at the bigger picture, you can better control emotions and behaviors and remain calm even in difficult situations or with people who trigger anger.

You can gradually work toward attaining inner peace by being mindful of thoughts, emotions, and actions while regularly practicing self-love. According to the first Reiki principle, "Just for today, I will not be angry," this belief eventually leads to living a more fulfilling life.

2. "Just for today, I will not worry."

The second Reiki principle encourages individuals to release their worries and focus on the present moment. This principle is "Just for today; I will not worry." This phrase helps people center on the present and let go of anxieties associated with overly worrying about the future or dwelling on the past.

When a person worries too much, it can lead to a negative mental state, and they can become trapped in their thoughts and struggles. It prevents them from fully embracing their lives and appreciating each moment as it occurs. Worrying can also cause physical stress, leading to headaches, stomachaches, fatigue, and other ailments complicating life. Reiki helps you break free from these patterns of worry by showing you how to be mindful of the present moment and take better care of yourself.

The phrase "Just for today, I will not worry" is an affirmation reminding you to stay in the present rather than ruminate on negative thoughts about the future or past events out of your control. Practicing this principle encourages individuals to live life intentionally instead of letting fear dictate their decisions or actions. It permits them to take time for themselves without feeling guilty or anxious, being kinder and gentler with themselves, so they have more energy for others.

3. "Just for today, I will do my work honestly."

The third Reiki principle is "Just for today; I will do my work honestly." This principle encourages being mindful of your intentions and motivations in your daily work. Taking ownership of your actions and being honest and ethical in everything you do is important. It enables you to build trust with others and ensure your actions positively impact those around you.

When doing honest work, remember to always act with integrity. It means being truthful in all interactions, taking responsibility for your mistakes, and not taking shortcuts or engaging in unethical practices like bribery or corruption. Your work will be of the highest quality. It will serve its intended purpose, maintaining a good reputation with those around you and building meaningful relationships based on mutual trust and respect.

Keeping your motivation pure when doing honest work is essential. You should strive to find joy in what you do rather than looking at it as a means toward an end or pursuing it solely out of greed or ambition. By working honestly, you help foster an environment of productivity, creativity, collaboration, and growth within yourself and those around you. You will inspire others to follow suit by setting a good example and demonstrating the value of hard work with integrity. This way, doing honest work creates a ripple effect by helping others reach their fullest potential.

4. "Just for today, be compassionate toward yourself and others."

The fourth Reiki principle is "Just for today, be compassionate toward yourself and others." This principle encourages self-compassion and kindness toward others, even when faced with difficulties. It calls you to set aside judgments and anger and focus on understanding others and your perspectives.

When practicing self-compassion, you accept your mistakes and shortcomings without excessive criticism or judgment. Additionally, self-compassion helps you work through difficult emotions healthily. When showing compassion toward others, you let go of feeling superior or inferior to them, recognizing that all people have flaws and no one is perfect. Compassion looks beyond these imperfections, helping you connect with one another more deeply.

Practicing self-compassion and compassion for others helps build resilience in times of adversity. When faced with challenging situations, you learn to respond with patience and understanding rather than judgment or anger and cope better with stressful life events. Furthermore, offering kindness and support to those in need benefits them and makes your life more meaningful.

5. "Just for today, I will be thankful for all my blessings."

The fifth Reiki principle is "Just for today; I will be thankful for all my blessings." This mantra encourages making a conscious effort to recognize and be grateful for your many blessings. By taking the time to appreciate what you have, you open up to the immense power of gratitude and abundance. Expressing thankfulness for life's simple pleasures, like a warm cup of tea or a sunny day, invites more of these moments into your life.

Gratitude helps cultivate positive emotions and relationships with others. Giving thanks and recognizing the good in those around you creates meaningful connections that could last a lifetime. Moreover, expressing gratitude allows you to better acknowledge daily successes and accomplishments, increasing satisfaction and motivation. It creates an attitude of abundance – not only material but spiritual abundance – which helps you to focus on what matters most.

Being thankful for all your blessings is a reminder that everything is fleeting and temporary. Life is full of ups and downs; it's important to recognize when times are good and savor them while they last. Gratitude helps keep life's minor problems in perspective by reminding you how much you have to be thankful for each day.

Can Reiki Be Self-Taught?

Reiki can be self-taught. However, many experts recommend working with an experienced practitioner if you are starting with this healing practice. Working with an experienced practitioner guides you on using Reiki for the best results and insight into what it means to become a Reiki practitioner. Nonetheless, some individuals have successfully learned how to do Reiki themselves through books, CDs, and other instructional materials available online or from specialty stores.

When practicing Reiki, remember everyone's experience is unique, and there is no one-size-fits-all approach to healing and balance. Each individual must find their way of connecting with the universal energy source when using this practice, whether through self-teaching methods or with an experienced Reiki master who helps guide their journey toward self-healing. Additionally, regular practice helps you become more attuned to your personal energy field, allowing you to effectively channel this energy for maximum benefit while treating yourself or others.

When learning Reiki, knowing it is all about energy flow is important. Therefore, developing an understanding of energy flow is key to mastering this technique. It can take time for your body to become attuned to the energy patterns of Reiki, but with proper training and commitment, you will eventually be able to manipulate this powerful force within yourself for healing purposes. Additionally, meditation practices benefit Reiki as they help put you in a relaxed state, allowing your body to open up more readily under its influence.

Anyone can learn to practice Reiki, whether they choose the traditional route by studying directly under a Master Teacher or teach themselves through books and other instructional resources available online and from specialty stores. Regardless, it takes dedication and commitment for someone seeking balance and wellness via this powerful modality to reap its full benefits, personally and professionally.

The Three Levels of Reiki

1. Shoden

Shoden is the first level of Reiki and the foundation of a Reiki practice. It introduces practitioners to Reiki and gives them a basic understanding of how it works and how to use it on themselves, other people, animals, plants, and objects.

During Shoden-level Reiki training, people learn more about energy healing, Reiki's history, its principles and etiquette (Rei-ki-ho), and the hand positions for self-treatment and treating others. Practitioners learn the power symbols used in treatments (Cho Ku Rei and Sei He Ki) and techniques for scanning the body for areas needing healing.

At this introductory level of learning, students are introduced to Dr. Mikao Usui's five principal teachings;

Just for today:

- Don't be angry
- Don't worry
- Be thankful
- Work hard
- Be kind to others

This teaching is integral to their training in understanding how to use Reiki and incorporate it into their daily lives.

The hands-on practice received at this level includes meditations where practitioners connect with their natural healing energy and Reiki methods on themselves by placing their hands in various positions on their body, sending Reiki energy through their hands. They receive instruction on how to treat others through touch or without touching by placing their hands a few inches away from someone's body while sending them healing energy.

In addition, practitioners are taught about personal boundaries when giving treatments and how to create a safe space for themselves and those they treat. By learning these basics during Shoden, practitioners develop a strong foundation serving them throughout future Reiki training levels.

2. Okuden

Okuden (intermediate level) is a level of Reiki building on the foundation of the Shoden (first level) teachings. It introduces more intricate concepts and practices, making practitioners more deeply attuned to their energy. This deeper understanding helps them to heal themselves and others better.

At the Okuden level, practitioners learn to use their life-force energy (ki) in healing processes. In addition, they learn techniques used to channel power from the universe into themselves and their clients, including focusing on a mental image or symbol when sending healing energy and focusing on an area of the body when performing treatments. They learn about the chakras and the auric field surrounding the body to identify healing or energizing areas.

Practitioners at the Okuden level will gain increased sensitivity to different energies and vibrations around them, allowing them to pick up on subtle clues during treatments indicating areas needing healing. At this stage, students learn techniques like long-distance healing to send Reiki energy over long distances without being physically present with their client.

The Okuden level is generally considered one of the most powerful levels of Reiki training available. Many practitioners feel it helps them to reach a new spiritual plane in their abilities. At this point, they connect with physical reality and unseen energies making up all aspects of existence – emotions, thoughts, and spirit. Mastering Okuden practitioners take responsibility for connecting with these higher spiritual energies and effectively moving forward in their chosen path toward self-mastery and personal growth.

3. Shinpiden

Shinpiden, known as the Master Level of Reiki, is the highest level of Reiki initiation. It involves a deep exploration of self-healing and energy awareness. At Shinpiden, practitioners receive three sacred symbols enhancing their healing capabilities and increasing their Reiki treatment power. This level allows practitioners to work with clients more profoundly, addressing deeper issues and blockages preventing them from living to their fullest potential.

At the Shinpiden level, practitioners gain an even greater understanding of using their Reiki energy combined with meditations, mantras, and affirmations for lasting results. They learn to identify energies hindering an individual's development or recovery from illness. Practitioners become masters of distance healing techniques, learning to connect with others spiritually regardless of physical proximity.

In addition to learning new symbols and techniques, Shinpiden practitioners are given specific tools to help them progress spiritually throughout life. These include communicating with higher guidance and creating powerful healing rituals or mantras to open up the pathways within themselves to tap into previously dormant spiritual powers. Practitioners are taught to access the Akashic Records containing all information about past lives and karmic patterns related to current life events.

Shinpiden students explore further aspects of Reiki, like spiritual counseling, kundalini activation, and soul retrieval, and advice on upholding spiritual boundaries when working with clients or conducting classes or workshops. Through this practice, they learn how best to work as conduits between the spirit world, natural elements, and humanity.

The journey taken at Shinpiden has been likened to completing a "spiritual apprenticeship" where a practitioner's true purpose is revealed. It helps them become conscious creators rather than victims of circumstances or limiting emotions and belief systems holding them back from achieving true happiness in this lifetime.

Chapter 6: Cleansing Energy with Reiki

Cleansing energy with Reiki is an incredibly powerful and research-backed tool to help improve physical, emotional, mental, and spiritual well-being. Your practitioner channels this special life energy into you to cleanse your aura and bring balance back into the body - allowing your cells access to more revitalizing vital force. This ancient practice is known to bring positive physical changes like increased energy levels, improved sleep patterns, and strengthened immune system functioning. Emotionally it can provide clarity of mind and less anxiety associated with stress. Mentally it offers better focus and clarity. Spiritually it nurtures peace, leading you toward your true life mission with unprecedented grace.

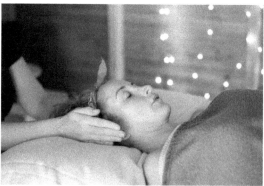

Reiki has the ability to cleanse any negative energy from your aura.
https://www.pexels.com/photo/crop-masseuse-with-hands-near-ears-of-woman-5240700/

How to Sense Energy through Reiki

Sensing energy is critical for Reiki practice, as practitioners can assess the energy flow in and around their clients. Understanding that everyone making up our world can feel or perceive subtle energies is important when beginning your journey into sensing energy. With practice, anyone can learn to detect and interpret this energy deeper.

The following exercises will help you become more proficient in sensing energy:

1. **Begin with an awareness meditation**: Sit comfortably in a quiet space, close your eyes, and focus on your breath. As thoughts arise, acknowledge them without judgment before gently returning your attention to your breathing. This exercise helps you become more mindful of your body and its sensations, allowing a heightened sense of awareness.

2. **Intentional grounding**: *Grounding* is connecting with the Earth's energy, helping you become more centered and connected to yourself and your environment. While seated or standing, place both feet firmly on the ground and shift your focus to this connection between yourself and the Earth. Visualize roots coming out of each foot as they travel down into the ground below. Once you feel connected, take deep breaths and relax into this feeling of stability.

3. **Scanning for energy**: Find a comfortable seated position or lie down in bed before slowly scanning your body for feelings that arise. You may feel sensations like warmth, tingling, or vibrations as you move your focus. If something stands out, pay closer attention to that area. As you do this exercise more often, you will recognize more subtle reactions and gain greater insight into the energy field surrounding your body.

4. **Connecting with others**: Stand or sit in a relaxed position with the person in front of you to practice sensing another person's energy field. Once connected with their presence through eye contact, release all expectations and become aware of feelings or impressions that arise within you during this connection. As time passes during this exchange, be open to the information you receive and pay attention to subtle changes in the energy you are sensing.

These simple steps will help you better understand the energy within yourself and others and become more proficient in using Reiki for healing purposes. Remember, practice makes perfect, so be patient with yourself as you explore this new realm of energy. With consistent effort and dedication, you can unlock the mysteries of Reiki energy.

Level 1-2 Reiki Techniques for Clearing Unwanted Energy from the Body

Pre Reiki Rituals

• Reiki Attunements

Reiki attunements, known as initiations, are essential in Reiki training. During an attunement ceremony, the Reiki practitioner enters a state of heightened receptivity so that they are open and receptive to Reiki's energy. Essentially, they are "tuned in" to the life force energy flowing through all living things. This tuning-in process enables them to access and transmit this powerful healing energy more easily and accurately.

• Using Reiki Symbols

Reiki symbols are integral to the Reiki healing practice and can help further deepen its effectiveness. They open and balance the energy channels in the body, allowing a more efficient flow of healing energy. The specific symbols used depend on the practitioner's tradition but typically include Cho Ku Rei, Sei He Ki, Hon Sha Ze Sho Nen, Dai Ko Myo, and Raku.

Cho Ku Rei is a symbol of power, protection, and grounding throughout Reiki sessions. It is believed to clear negative energy from an aura or environment and strengthen the connection to their higher self.

Cho Ku Rei.

Chokurei.jpg: Stephen Buck The Reiki Sanghaderivative work: LeonardoelRojo, CC BY-SA 2.0 <https://creativecommons.org/licenses/by-sa/2.0>, via Wikimedia Commons https://commons.wikimedia.org/wiki/File:Chokurei.svg

Sei He Ki helps promote mental clarity while aiding in emotional healing. It is a particularly powerful symbol for helping process emotions a person has difficulty working through without assistance.

Sei He Ki.

Hon Sha Ze Sho Nen assists in distance healing by creating an energetic bridge between two people so they benefit from a session, even if they are not physically with each other.

Hon Sha Ze Sho Nen.

Dai Ko Myo represents spiritual enlightenment and helps you to open up a deeper understanding of yourself.

Dai Ko Myo.
Nathaniel_U's, CC BY 2.0

Raku encourages growth and transformation in life by viewing yourself from a place of non-judgmental acceptance.

Using these symbols during practice can help amplify the power of Reiki and help clear energy blocks in the body or mind. They are used before starting a session or as needed throughout to break up stagnant energies getting in the way of successful healing. When these symbols are used with intention, their effectiveness increases exponentially, so focus on them when invoking these special tools in your practice.

Steps for Cleansing Unwanted Energies

Reiki Breath and Visualization Technique

The Reiki Breath technique is a gentle and effective way of clearing unwanted energy from your body or another's. It is a simple yet powerful tool for clearing obstructions in the body in just a few minutes. Here are the steps to guide you through this technique:

1. Sit or lie down comfortably with your feet resting flat on the floor or ground. You can close or open your eyes, whichever feels more comfortable.

2. Take several deep breaths to relax, become aware of your intuition, and visualize a white light entering your body. Sink into this visualization and focus on feeling love and peace radiating throughout your being.

3. Once you have taken several deep breaths, imagine the negative energy in your body being released through your breath - thoughts, emotions, physical pain, etc. See this energy evaporating from you until it has completely dissipated from your being.

4. After releasing your negative energy, you can extend Reiki healing to others. Visualize a white light emanating from the center of your heart chakra and extending outward like fingers around someone's body whom you want to help heal - even if they are not with you physically - until it envelopes them in a loving embrace of light and warmth. Use other colors of light depending on the healing.

5. Allow yourself to imagine negative energy or obstructions within their bodies releasing through their breath. At the same time, they, too, take deep breaths - see them in their relaxed state with no pain or discomfort before slowly opening your eyes, feeling refreshed and revitalized.

Reiki Hand Position Technique

The next step is using the Reiki hand position technique, a powerful way to clear unwanted energy from the body.

1. After completing the visualization, take a few deep breaths to become fully present and relaxed.

2. When you feel ready, place your hands in various positions on the body – like the abdomen, chest, back, or head. With each position, take time to sense sensations that arise. Do not try to control these sensations but allow them to move through you. Move slowly and feel the energy entering your hands.

3. Once you have placed your hands in each position, gently move them in small circles or waves on the area for around 3-5 minutes. It helps clear out unwanted energy from the person's body, allowing space for healing energies to enter.

4. Furthermore, it is important not to apply too much pressure while moving your hands; instead, allow yourself to be guided by

whatever feels right at each moment. Trust that Reiki knows how to balance the energies of the person's body best.

• Hand Positions for Self-Cleansing

The Prayer Position: Simply bring both hands together in front of your heart center. Press your palms firmly against each other and your fingertips pointing toward the sky. It creates a powerful energetic connection between both hands, acting as a bridge between the physical and the spiritual world, allowing you to draw out stuck energy which may be obstructing your energy flow. This position is ideal for anyone looking to create balance within their system or open up blocked chakras.

The Open Palm Position: Sit with your spine straight and extend both arms directly out in front of you at shoulder height, palms facing outward. Take slow deep breaths while visualizing yourself, sending healing light from your fingertips into the environment. As you exhale, imagine negative or stuck energy being pulled out through your palms and back into the environment where it will be transmuted away from your system forever. This position helps expand your energetic fields while providing protection from outside influences that might otherwise interfere with your vibrations.

The Palms Down Position: Sit comfortably with arms extended forward at shoulder height, palms facing down toward the ground beneath you. Imagine roots growing out from each fingertip into the Earth below, where they can draw in nurturing energies while simultaneously drawing out heavy or stagnant energy built up over time within your system. This exercise helps connect deeply to Mother Earth's nourishing embrace while promoting grounding and stability on all mental, emotional, and physical levels.

• Hand Position for Cleansing Another Person's Energies

You can use numerous hand positions to clear unwanted energy from another person's body. Each position facilitates different aspects of the energy-clearing process, from focusing on specific areas to creating a more comprehensive clearing effect.

One of the most basic hand positions for energy cleansing is placing one or both hands hovering an inch over the person's chakras or energy centers. It helps clear out stagnant or stuck energy in those areas. Visualizing a particular color –pink, blue, or green – associated with healing and cleansing as you use this technique can be beneficial.

Another popular hand position requires cupping your hands around the person's head and shoulders while taking deep breaths together. Combine this technique with visualizing a healing light entering through your palms and into your body. This technique helps create overall balance and well-being.

Use your hands to massage tension points in the person's body, such as their back, neck, and shoulders. Gently massaging these areas helps release built-up stress and tension, allowing more positive energy to flow through them unhindered. You could add soothing aromatherapy oils for extra relaxation benefits.

Grounding

The Reiki grounding technique to clear unwanted energy is creating a grounding cord.

Take a few moments to concentrate and refocus.

1. Close your eyes and take several deep breaths. Feel your feet on the floor and imagine being connected to the Earth's energy through its core.

2. Visualize a grounding cord extending from the base chakra, at the base of your spine, down into the earth below you. This cord should be visible in whatever form or color feels natural; some people imagine it as a thick rope, others as an electrical wire.

3. Focus on feeling connected with this energy so that all excess or unwanted energies can be pulled out through this cord and back into the earth, transmuted into light and love.

4. Once you have established your grounding cord, place your hands over the area of concern (yourself or another person) for about three minutes. Stay present in your breath throughout this process. It is important to stay aware of what is happening within you and in the environment around you.

5. If needed, silently ask for guidance from higher sources or spiritual beings offering assistance during this session.

After completing step five, slowly release the tension held throughout this process by slowly exhaling until feeling more relaxed before beginning future steps in this clearing process. It is beneficial to thank spiritual entities who assisted you during the session before finishing with self-care, like a cup of tea or walking outside in nature.

Final Release

The final release is the final step in cleansing unwanted energies from your or another's body. Take a few deep breaths and ground yourself, visualizing excess or unwanted energies leaving the body through a white light. It is essential to give gratitude for the Reiki healing and thank the Reiki energy for aiding in cleansing unwanted energies, as this could be a crucial part of spiritual healing.

Next, moving into a relaxed state and letting yourself settle into stillness is important. If desired, take this time to reflect on your experience and write down what you experienced during the healing process journals. Your journals will allow you to reflect on your journey toward spiritual growth and development, so take some time to recognize what you have learned during the process of releasing energy.

Finally, end your session with meditation or contemplation. Focus on your breathing patterns and allow yourself to be surrounded by stillness while holding positive thoughts. Do not forget to remain grateful for all you have learned during this journey - self-reflection can lead to a further understanding of innermost thoughts, desires, beliefs, and values. You will feel energized or refreshed when you finish. Whatever emotions you feel in that moment are valid and should be embraced fully before returning to reality with a renewed awareness.

Can Reiki Cleanse Unblocked Chakras?

A Reiki cleanse is a great way to unblock chakras. Reiki combines touch and meditation to help bring balance and harmony to the body's energy systems. During a Reiki cleanse, the practitioner uses their hands in specific positions over the chakras corresponding with each chakra's energy centers. The practitioner allows the energy flow to be released from these chakra points, clearing blockages or disruption, using the healing power of Reiki's universal life force energy throughout the entire body, including the chakras.

The chakras are essential for physical and emotional health, as they control the ability to connect energetically. When one or more chakras become blocked, it can cause a number of issues ranging from physical pain and illness to mental health problems like anxiety and depression. A Reiki cleanse can help clear obstructions built up over time while restoring proper balance throughout all seven chakras. It helps clear negative emotions and feelings trapped within you due to life experiences or traumas, so you can move forward more positively with renewed energy and joy.

Reiki is a powerful healing modality facilitating physical, emotional, mental, and spiritual well-being. It helps individuals reconnect with their deepest essence - their true self - increasing overall peace and joy to live an empowered life filled with purposeful intention. Unblocking energetic blocks within the chakras through regular Reiki cleanses individuals and creates a foundation for lasting health on all levels; mind, body, soul, and spirit.

Chapter 7: To Smudge or Not to Smudge

You don't know what to do. To smudge or not to smudge? This is an important decision, as smudging is a powerful spiritual practice. Smudging is burning sacred herbs and resins, like sage, cedar, sweetgrass, and lavender, to purify and cleanse the energy of a space. Many cultures have specific traditions for smudging, often involving prayer or other rituals. For example, in some Native American cultures, sweetgrass braids are lit and used for smudging to release the sacred plant's positive energy into the air. Whatever your reason for wanting to cleanse an area spiritually, smudging may be just the thing.

Smudging is a process that has been used by many cultures for different spiritual purposes.
https://unsplash.com/photos/x5hyhMBjR3M

Is Smudging Closed Practice or a Cultural Appropriation?

Smudging, a sacred practice of burning herbs or resins to purify a space, has been popularized in recent years. This practice is often associated with Native American cultures. Many spiritual and new-age practitioners consider it a closed practice, meaning it should only be used by those within the culture with the right knowledge and understanding of its importance.

In addition to being considered a closed practice, some claim that smudging has become an example of cultural appropriation (when one culture takes elements from another without permission or understanding the original context). It includes adopting symbols from other cultures or attempting to pass off traditional practices as their own. For example, many people learn about smudging from books, TV shows, and movies rather than through traditional teachings without full knowledge of its spiritual significance and implications.

The controversy surrounding smudging has grown over the past few years as more non-natives attempt to use it for their spiritual practices without fully understanding its history and significance. For example, celebrities like Gwyneth Paltrow have posted photos on social media performing smudges in their homes. It may be harmless enough at face value, but if done without proper respect for the tradition, it can be seen as appropriative behavior.

However, not all non-natives engaging in smudging do it out of disrespect – many individuals find real spiritual benefit in its use – but even those with good intentions can cause harm if they do not properly respect the traditions. When engaging with smudging, it's crucial for anyone who is not part of the culture to take time to research its history, understand its significance within Native American contexts, ask permission when appropriate, and give credit where due when sharing information. It helps prevent the practice from being appropriated or trivialized by those outside its traditions and ensures native voices are heard when discussing issues around these spiritual practices.

The Difference between Smudging and Smoke Cleansing

Smudging and smoke cleansing are ancient spiritual rituals used for centuries to cleanse and protect people, places, and objects. While both use smoke to purify, the two practices have some distinct differences.

Smudging is a ritual practice dating back thousands of years and is most commonly associated with Native American culture. It uses a bundle of sage, sweetgrass, cedar, tobacco, or other dried herbs to create an incense-like substance. This smudge is lit until it creates smoke, which cleanses the area or person of negative energy. Smudging is often used for prayer, meditation, and connecting with the spirit world.

On the other hand, smoke cleansing or fumigation has its roots in many ancient cultures, including Greek, Roman, and African traditions. It involves burning specific herbs like frankincense or sandalwood over charcoal tablets to produce a large amount of fragrant smoke. This smoke purifies an environment or object by clearing out stagnant energy or negative influences while simultaneously healing emotional wounds and restoring balance in the body's energy field.

Smudging and smoke cleansing both use fragrant smoke to purify an area or object, but they differ primarily in their origin stories and ingredients when performing the rituals. Smudging often uses bundles of dried herbs, whereas smoke cleansing utilizes specific herbs like frankincense or sandalwood burned over charcoal tablets. Smudging typically serves spiritual purposes related to prayer or connecting with the spirit world. Smoke cleansing primarily focuses on healing emotional wounds and restoring balance in energy fields rather than invoking spiritual guidance.

Benefits of Smoke Cleansing

Smoke cleansing is an ancient practice used by many indigenous cultures and Shamans for centuries. They believe it is a powerful way to clear negative energy and create balance and harmony in a space. Smoke cleansing involves burning natural herbs such as sage, cedar, sweetgrass, copal, lavender, or palo santo, which release fragrant smoke into the air. As the smoke travels through the air, it has the power to cleanse a space of negative energies, creating positive feelings and raising vibration.

One of the greatest benefits of smoke cleansing is its ability to help reduce stress and anxiety, usually through the calming effects of its smell. The pleasant aroma released by burning herbs like sage or cedar helps promote relaxation and calmness in the body and mind. Additionally, this smell can inspire creativity due to its potential ability to heighten your senses.

Smoke cleansing has also been proven to have antiseptic properties. It can effectively purify the air in a room with viruses or bacteria causing respiratory issues or illnesses like colds and flu. Therefore, it is an ideal way to disinfect indoor spaces without using harmful chemicals or sprays. Furthermore, smoke cleansing can improve concentration due to its soothing aroma helping to foster a relaxing atmosphere, perfect for studying or working on tasks requiring greater focus and attention span.

Another key benefit of smoke cleansing is its spiritual aspect. It is believed that when practiced in sacred ceremonies, besides clearing built-up negative energies, it attracts positive intentions from the universe, allowing you to manifest your desires more easily. In addition, by focusing on each herb during your ritual, you can connect with its medicinal properties, which are healing agents for physical, emotional, and mental health issues like inflammation and depression.

Smoke cleansing is beneficial because it encourages mindful presence during rituals, actively engaging all five senses; sight (seeing), sound (hearing), smell (smelling), taste (tasting), and touch (feeling). This mindful practice helps bring awareness into your daily life, helping you stay connected with your surroundings while developing greater self-awareness along the journey.

Many incredible benefits are associated with smoke cleansing:

- Reducing stress levels and anxiety
- Improving concentration
- Purifying air
- Drawing positive intentions from the universe
- Aiding physical, emotional, and mental health healing
- Encouraging mindfulness

It is an invaluable ritual for anyone seeking spiritual growth and personal development.

Types of Smoke Cleansing

A herb combination for smoke cleansing is the traditional Native American smudging practice, which uses four main herbs; white sage, sweetgrass, cedar, and lavender. White sage spiritually cleanses an area by driving out negative energy. Sweetgrass helps bring in positive energy. Cedar purifies a space, protects against bad luck, and promotes longevity. Lavender helps promote relaxation and peace of mind. By burning these herbs together, the smoke created can cleanse a person or room of negative energies and protect them from harm.

Another herb combination often used for smoke cleansing is palo santo wood, from South America, where it's traditionally used in shamanic healing ceremonies. When burned, this wood produces a fragrant smoke, which helps purify an environment by reducing negative energy, stress, and anxiety, promoting calmness, peace, and enlightenment. Palo santo wood helps people connect with their higher selves during meditation or prayer rituals by aiding in reaching deeper levels of consciousness.

Finally, many cultures worldwide use herbal mixtures for smoke-cleansing purposes, including frankincense and myrrh from Ethiopia and Copal from Guatemala, among others. Frankincense was traditionally burned as incense to cleanse spaces and ward off evil spirits or bad luck. The aroma of burning this resin helps clear away negative energy, allowing those present to feel relaxed, comforted, and safe in their surroundings. Myrrh has long been associated with religious ceremonies due to its strong aromatic scent, and it aids in connecting with a higher power. Burning this resin encourages reverence, creating an atmosphere conducive to meditation or prayer. Copal is another tree resin whose smoke has been used for spiritual purification ceremonies since ancient times. Its fragrant aroma is known to drive away negativity, simultaneously protecting against evil influences.

How to Create Your Smudge Stick

Creating your smudge stick is quite straightforward, but it requires patience and a good amount of research. Before you start, double-check if the herbs you use are safe to burn. Some plants contain oils or toxins that can be dangerous when burned in an enclosed space. Additionally, be mindful of allergic reactions – some people are sensitive to certain plants.

When picking herbs for your smudge stick, opt for more accessible herbs, such as white sage (*Salvia apiana*), cedar (*Juniperus virginiana*), mugwort (*Artemesia vulgaris*), lavender (*Lavandula angustifolia*), and rosemary (*Rosmarinus officinalis*). These herbs have an array of benefits, from protection and cleansing to healing.

Here are the steps to make your smudge stick once you've chosen your herbs:

1. Gather long branches or stems of herbs and bundle them together with a string. Leave enough space between each herb so air can circulate throughout the bundle.

2. Securely tie the string into a knot at one end, then wrap it around the middle of the bundle several times before tying it off again on the other end.

3. To dry the smudge stick, hang it in a warm, well-ventilated area like a garage or porch for two weeks. Turn it over every other day so the herbs will dry evenly.

4. When your smudge stick is completely dry, it is ready to burn. You can light it directly with a match, or if you want more control over the smoke, place a bowl of sand and charcoal underneath the smudge stick.

When burning your smudge stick, you must keep an eye on the embers and put out any that are too big. Never leave the burning herb unattended for long periods because of fire hazard risks. Remember to dispose of the ashes properly in a metal container filled with sand or water when the ritual is finished.

Creating your smudge stick can be a rewarding and spiritual experience, as it is an ancient ritual used to ward off negative energy, cleanse the home, and bring in positive vibes. However, it's important to research beforehand and ensure your herbs are safe to burn. If you want to learn more about various herbs and plants for this purpose, take a peek at the chapter glossary of herbs at the end of this book for further information.

Types of Smudge Sticks

There are many different smudge sticks, each with unique properties and uses.

1. **White Sage Smudge Stick:** White sage is a common smudge stick for cleansing and purifying. It is usually burned as incense or added to other herbs for deeper cleansing. This sage has a strong, pungent smell and is used to clear the air of negative energy.

2. **Cedar Smudge Stick:** Cedar is another popular choice for smudging and has similar purposes as white sage. The cedar's scent is earthy and sweet, helping to promote grounding and safety in the home or office space. In some Native American tribes, cedar was used to bring prosperity and success into the home.

3. **Mugwort Smudge Stick:** Mugwort is less commonly known than white sage or cedar but has been used in various cultures since ancient times. The smoke of burning mugwort carries healing properties to help with lucid dreaming and healing emotional trauma. It protects from harmful energies when burned indoors or outdoors.

4. **Palo Santo Smudge Stick:** *Palo santo* comes from South America and is made from fragrant wood pieces of trees found in Peru, Ecuador, Mexico, and Guatemala. The smoke of burning palo santo has spiritual cleansing powers to help clear negative energy from space when burned regularly. It has a more pleasant aroma than other smudge sticks, making it perfect for aromatherapy and spiritual cleansing rituals.

5. **Sweetgrass:** Sweetgrass is an herb native to North America that's often used in sacred ceremonies because it invokes gratitude and positivity in those who experience its fragrance. Sweetgrass helps clear away negative energy and brings blessings into the environment where it's being burned.

How to Cleanse Yourself

Start by creating an environment of peace and tranquility. You can achieve this through essential oils, like lavender or chamomile, dimming the lights, playing soft music, burning incense, or other measures that help create a calming atmosphere.

Next, take deep breaths to relax your body and mind. As you breathe in, imagine all positive energy entering your body, leaving you feeling relaxed and refreshed. As you breathe out, imagine releasing all the negativity away from you. Continue until you are in a completely tranquil state.

Now, it is time to open your aura and release all the stagnant energy. Recite the affirmation: *"I open my aura and release all stagnation within it."* Visualize a powerful light radiating from the center of your chest, slowly expanding and cleansing your energy field. Do this until you feel your aura is completely clear of negative energy.

The next step is to recite positive affirmations or prayers. You can do these silently or aloud, depending on what resonates with you best. Some examples of positive affirmations include, *"I am worthy of love and happiness"* or *"My life is full of abundance and gratitude."* Some traditional prayers are The Lord's Prayer, The Hail Mary, or Psalm 23.

In addition to affirmations and prayers, using sound can cleanse and balance the energy fields. Examples of sounds to help with cleansing include singing bowls, tuning forks, bells, or clapping hands. These tools vibrate your energy field, allowing stagnant energy to dissipate.

Herbal remedies are popular for cleansing yourself spiritually. Many herbs have properties to help open up the heart chakra, allowing for love, acceptance, and healing to enter your life. Common herbs used in cleansing include lavender, sage, rosemary, jasmine, and mint. You can use these herbs by burning them during meditation or ritual practices, drinking them as teas or infusions, or carrying them around with you when you need a reminder that you are on a spiritual journey.

Finally, closing your aura once you're finished with the cleansing ritual is important. Take deep breaths and visualize a powerful light radiating from the center of your chest, slowly shrinking until all your energy is fully contained within it. Affirm, *"My aura is closed, and I am protected,"* as you do this visualization. It helps keep negative energies away, so you remain in an open state for positive energies.

Following these simple steps, you can successfully cleanse yourself and remain in a state of peace and positivity. Remember to include positive affirmations and prayers, and use sound to maximize the effects. Lastly, take time to appreciate yourself for participating in this cleansing ritual and express gratitude for everything you have achieved.

Regularly cleanse yourself to benefit from the inner peace and clarity of releasing negativity and inviting more positivity into your life.

How to Cleanse Your Home

Cleansing your home is vital in spiritual practice. Cleansing can help clear stagnant energy and bring in fresh, positive vibrations. It helps create safety, peace, and comfort in your home. Follow these steps to cleanse your home:

1. **Clear the air:** Open the windows and doors to allow fresh air inside. Light incense or sage sticks fill the space with cleansing smoke. If you have essential oils available, you can use them, too. Mix two drops of jasmine, lavender, and lemon essential oil in a diffuser for a soothing scent with purifying benefits.

2. **Create a mantra:** Focus on the intention of clearing away negative energy and inviting positive vibrations into your home. Create a simple mantra you can repeat to yourself, such as *"My home is full of love and light"* or *"All negativity be gone from my space."*

3. **Visualize:** Take a few moments to close your eyes and visualize all the energies in your home released through the open windows and doors. Imagine white or gold light entering your home with fresh air and filling every corner of your space with peacefulness.

4. **Use sound:** Singing bowls, chimes, tuning forks, drums, or other instruments are great tools for cleansing spaces energetically. You can use traditional chants like Om and the Gayatri Mantra to bless your home with positivity.

5. **Pray:** Offer a prayer or affirmation of gratitude and ask for protection from negative energies. Light a candle and focus on sending love into your home, then blow out the flame to signal the completion of this cleansing stage.

6. **Cleanse crystals:** Crystals have special properties that energetically cleanse homes, so if you have them in your space, it's important to clear them periodically. Place each crystal in sea salt overnight and rinse it off the next day. This will help remove the buildup of energy absorbed over time.

7. **Focus on self-care**: Take the time to treat yourself kindly. Spend time in meditation or relax and connect with your breath. It will help you remain grounded and centered after cleansing your

home.

8. **Seal it:** To finish your ritual, smudge around the four corners of each room with incense or sage smoke, then seal the doorways with salt to keep negative energy out and protect your sacred space. You can use a quartz crystal in each corner for added protection.

9. **Give Thanks:** Take a few moments to thank the universe for all you have and the cleansing energy within your home. Feel free to add prayers, affirmations, sounds, essential oils, or other items that feel right for your space. When you have finished, take one final deep breath and relax into the positive energy in your cleansed space.

How to Cleanse a Negative Object

Cleansing an object can be a powerful way to reclaim the energy and space within your home. It is important to do this ritual to protect yourself from negative energies that might have been left behind. Cleansing an object uses various methods, such as prayers, affirmations, sounds, essential oils, smudging with herbs or incense, visualization with or without candles, or chanting. Here are step-by-step instructions for cleansing an object:

1. Start by physically cleaning the object. Make sure it is free of dirt and dust before you move on to other cleansing techniques.

2. Select a prayer or affirmation that resonates with you and speak aloud while focusing on the object Examples of prayers or affirmations; *"I cleanse this object of all energy that does not belong to me," "I fill this space with positive, loving energy."*

3. Use a sound tool like a drum or crystal singing bowl and create a vibration around the object. It will help release the negative energy attached to it.

4. Smudge the object with herbs or incense, such as sage, cedar, sweetgrass, or palo santo wood. As you smudge around the object, focus on releasing the negative energies left behind and invite peace and love.

5. Visualize the object surrounded by a white light or energy field protecting it from unwanted energies. You can use candles around the object to help create an inviting space.

6. Chant mantras or words of power that are meaningful to you while focusing on the object. It will help raise its vibration and invite positive energy into your home.

7. Place drops of essential oils, such as lavender, frankincense, or sandalwood, on the object for added protection and cleansing benefits.

8. Finally, thank your spiritual source for helping cleanse this object and set a clear intention of how you want to use it in the future.

By following these cleansing techniques, you can be confident the object has been cleansed of negative energy and is ready for use in your home. Remember, stay mindful of how you use the object to prevent unwanted energies from returning to your space. May peace, love, and light be with you.

Chapter 8: Spiritual Baths for Cleansing and Protection

Baths have been part of spiritual practices since ancient times. They were known for their healing, cleansing, and protective properties and their ability to relieve stress and anxiety symptoms and improve overall well-being. People in ancient times felt drawn to water subconsciously. They understood that water was essential for survival and acknowledged its spiritual healing properties. Bathing was a regular custom in Ancient Greece, India, Israel, and Egypt. In most of these cultures, bathing was known as purification by water, especially if bathed in salt water. The most primitive forms of this practice included visiting springs known for healing practice and submerging in water as an expression of devotion to their faith. Drawing on a bath with stones and salt was developed later as part of spiritual pursuits. The added salt or rock water enhanced the water's cleansing properties, and people gladly took advantage of it.

If this is the first time you've heard of a spiritual bath, you aren't alone. However, many people take spiritual baths before even realizing they've existed. For example, if you took a bath longer than necessary to get clean, you've already stepped into this spiritual practice. If you prefer baths over showers, you already know nothing compares to soaking in a hot, soothing bath after a busy day. Many people enjoy taking their time reading, listening to music, or sipping a glass of wine while soaking. They might even light a candle or two. They let the water and the stillness of the moment relax them. However, spiritual baths are slightly different.

They require an intention and an active approach to relaxing. Otherwise, you cannot focus on your intent, and your bath rituals won't be as effective as when you channel your intention. The key to performing this spiritual exercise is knowing what you expect from your time in the water. As you submerge your entire body, your intention channels the energies you want to work on. Therefore, lie down and soak yourself well while repeating your intentions.

The best characteristic of spiritual baths is you can always put your spin on them. This chapter provides instructions for baths for spiritual cleansing and protection, but you're free to alter them to your liking. You can infuse them with other preferred spiritual tools to boost the effectiveness of your intention and nourish it until its manifests into reality.

The Purpose of Spiritual Baths

A spiritual bath is a magnificent way to refresh your body, mind, and soul. You can supply your body, mind, and soul with healing energy, allowing them to protect you from harmful influences. You've probably noticed that you feel different after taking a regular bath than you did before - your sense of rejuvenation and calmness goes beyond your body. Due to their ingredients, spiritual baths can amplify this feeling. These ingredients often contain unique energies or compounds affecting your energy. They have different purposes, which you can use in a spiritual bath with specific intent.

The primary purpose of spiritual baths is to give yourself time to reflect on the sensation enveloping your body and those that go beyond. During a spiritual bath, inspect your emotions in the present moment. Taking the time and space to ground yourself enables you to identify areas in your body, mind, and spirit that could benefit from energetic healing.

While you examine the problematic areas, seek inspiration for working on them through other means. Therefore, spiritual baths are not only cleansing and protective, but they're also centering and motivating. They can take you closer to nature and be grateful for its gifts, including the water and all the natural ingredients in your bath.

Another purpose of spiritual baths is to balance the chakras, which heal your mind, body, and soul. Clearing blockages from the chakras contributes to their healthy function and ability to prevent illnesses and injuries.

The Benefits of Spiritual Baths

A spiritual bath can have different benefits depending on your ingredients and intention. Typically, spiritual baths purify one energetic field and cleanse the body, mind, and spirit. Other benefits include:

- **Lessening the effects of external stimuli**: In this fast-paced world, you are constantly bombarded with information. The environments you move in, the people you deal with, and the entertainment you consume are all packed with stimuli affecting your energies. Spiritual baths can help lower the energy imprint of those influences disrupting your balance.

- **Relax the nervous system:** Many ingredients in spiritual baths can soothe irritated nerves, restore hormone balance affecting the nervous system, and reduce the effects of negative emotions. It has a wholesome influence on your overall health. After a stressful day, you can take a bath to tune out all your worries and enjoy a soothing atmosphere.

- **Flushing out toxins**: Soaking in the bathtub with salt water or other ingredients with antioxidative effects is as effective as drinking detox drinks. Moreover, a bath takes less time to prepare and has less potential for unwanted effects on your body. By spending only 20 minutes in a bathtub, you'll flush out all the toxins in your body and promote your well-being.

- **Creating the perfect atmosphere for contemplation:** Since you're already relaxing and cleansing in your bathtub, you can use the time for a little reflective investigation of yourself. You can ponder your intention or think about your goals and desires; the latter practice is excellent for establishing a connection between your intuition and your spiritual self. You can use any exercise to gain more self-awareness and reveal your innermost needs.

- **Purifying the energetic body**: Spiritual baths have a therapeutic effect on balancing your subtle energies. They replace stagnant or harmful energy with positive vibes and raise your vibrations. Salts, crystals, and essential oils are essential for cleansing your energetic body. Essential oils will help you replace the flushed-out energy with renewed energy, especially if you spend at least 25-30 minutes soaking and relaxing in the tub.

How to Take a Spiritual Bath

There are no instructions on how to take a spiritual bath. However, you should always use an intention and ingredients that fit your current needs. Regardless of your goal, you can take a few steps to make your baths more effective. Infusing your bath with the most appropriate intention is crucial, granting you a greater experience.

Instructions:

1. **Ensure your bathtub is clean before you take a bath.** Otherwise, the residual negative energy can interfere with the bath rituals, reducing their effectiveness. Whether you want cleansing, protection, or healing, the number one rule is to start with a clean slate. Cleaning the bathtub and the surrounding area helps eliminate harmful influences from your bathroom and allows your baths to take full effect.

2. **You can play music.** It can be meditation music or music that helps you relax and adds to the bath's spiritual cleansing and protection benefits. Alternatively, you can listen to a guided meditation while you soak. Or, if you're confident enough, you can sing before and after the bath. The latter helps clear the space from negative energies that have exited your body, mind, and spirit while soaking.

3. **Stay unplugged.** The ability to listen to music or sounds doesn't mean you should be on your phone or use other electronic devices while soaking. Place any device playing the audio as far away from your reach as possible to remain "unplugged."

4. **Set a clear intent.** Whether you want your energetic pathways cleansed, resolve negative situations, cleanse your body, mind, and spirit, or attract positive influences into your life, define it clearly before you prepare for your bath.

5. **Take your time** reflecting on how you feel before and after taking a bath. Not all cleansing baths work for everyone. To see if a particular bath works for you, acknowledge what you need help with and compare your results to how you felt before taking it.

6. **When using essential oils and herbs, you must be familiar with their effects.** Not all herbs and oils are safe for everyone, particularly on your skin, and only use those recommended for baths. If you notice an adverse reaction, stop using them in your baths.

Bath to Reinforce Your Psychic Defenses

This is the right bath for you if you feel vulnerable to negative influences and need empowerment to attract positive energy. It will reinforce your psychic defenses, helping you ward off negative energies and keep your chakras balanced and healthy. It uses Himalayan salt, known for its ability to deter negative energy, drawing it away from the body and the toxins causing the negative energy accumulation. If you have this option, take a bath next to an open window at full moon to let the moonlight bless you while you soak.

Ingredients:

- Blessed water (or water charged with spiritual energy from crystals, the moon, etc.)
- Essential oils or other plant-based scents
- Candles
- Herbs - fresh or dry
- Incense
- Crystals
- Himalayan salt
- Tea bags
- Moonlight (optional)
- Relaxing music (optional)

Instructions:

1. Set the appropriate mood in your bathroom. Light several candles around the bathtub and turn off the artificial lights. You can light incense and turn on relaxing music.

2. Consider your intention. Think about what you want to achieve from this bath and how you can help your mind and spirit improve your psychic defenses. Focus on your intention.

3. Fill your bathtub with water at the appropriate temperature and add the cleansing ingredients. You can use as many or as few as you like.

4. When the tub is filled, get in the water. As you enjoy soaking, concentrate on taking deep breaths. Feel how the air moves through your body.

5. Consider how you feel when breathing. Notice if any part of your body is affected by negative energies. Visualize the healing effects of the bath, clearing up these problematic areas. If it helps, meditate before you delve into visualization.

6. Soak as long as needed, dipping your head under the water several times during your bath. When ready, exit the bathtub and dry yourself. Use a moisturizing agent after your cleansing bath.

7. If you've used only natural ingredients in your bath, take some bath water and offer it back to nature. Thank it for its help in cleansing you of negative energies. You can pour it into your garden or pots for your houseplants.

Salt Water Bath to Ward Off the Evil Eye

Saltwater baths have plenty of benefits. They can relieve stress, pain, and fatigue, improve circulation, and cleanse the chakra system. They're known to draw out toxins from the body, exfoliate the body, reduce skin irritation, and heal minor injuries. A lesser-known effect of salt bath waters is their ability to ward off the evil eye. While sea salt is the most effective for this purpose, you can use coarse sea salt if you don't have it available. It's an incredibly simple and ineffective method to ensure you'll never be affected by this curse and mal-intent.

Ingredients:

- Rock or coarse sea salt
- Lavender or tea tree essential oil
- A bucket
- Lukewarm water

Instructions:

1. Pour water into a bucket until half full. Add the salt and a few drops of essential oils to the water. Stir until the salt has

completely dissolved.

2. Stand in your bathtub and slowly pour the salt water over your body, from head to toe. Avoid getting water in your eyes. Feel how it's cleansing you of negative energies.

3. Once you've finished with the salt bath, wash your hair and body with natural soap and shampoo. The salt can dry out your skin and hair, so you must replenish the nutrients-moisture immediately after the bath.

4. You can repeat the bath 2-3 times a week, depending on how strong your defense needs to ward off the evil eye.

Chakra-Balancing Ritual Bath

Balancing the energies in your chakras is crucial for attaining optimal spiritual health. You can balance your chakra bath and improve its energy-flowing capacities with a customized chakra bath. Use crystals, oils, and herbs associated with the chakra you want to balance. It's recommended to focus on balancing one chakra at a time.

Ingredients:

- Stones associated with a specific chakra
- Herbs linked to different chakras
- 8-10 drops of essential oils associated with a specific chakra
- 1 cup of Epsom or Himalayan salt
- Candles
- Colored light bulbs (optional)
- Music to relax (optional)

Instructions:

1. Cleanse your crystals before placing them on the edge of the tub. Clean them by smudging, putting them into a bowl of salt, or leaving them outside your window at full moon.

2. If you're using dried herbs, brew a strong tea with them first.

3. When ready, run the bath. If the stones are small, put them in a small pouch when placing them on the tub's edge so you don't lose them.

4. Place candles around the tub and light them. Put on relaxing music if it helps you calm down so you can focus on your

cleansing intent.

5. Add the oils, salt, and herbal teas to the water and stir to combine. When everything is combined, get in, and enjoy your bath.

Pain-Pain-Go-Away Bath

Dealing with constant pain and fatigue negatively affects your chakras and your spiritual balance. You can restore your energetic balance and improve your overall health with a bath designed to make your aches go away.

Ingredients:

- Essential oils - chamomile, lavender, and rosemary work best or
- Dried herbs in infusion bags or fresh herbs
- Honey
- Oat milk
- Rice
- Dead sea salt
- Exfoliant for body and face

Instructions:

1. Fill your bathtub. Adjust the water temperature to your preference. While the tub is filling up, prepare the rest of the ingredients.

2. Mix 10-20 drops of essential oil and the rest of the ingredients in a medium bowl. Scale the ingredients according to your preferences, but you should create a homogeneous mixture.

3. Add the mixture to your bath and stir the water for even distribution. Get in and enjoy soaking for at least 20 minutes.

4. Before getting out, use an exfoliant on your body and face to deep clean your skin and activate a healthy flow of positive energy in your body, mind, and soul.

Rejuvenating Bath

There is nothing better than feeling refreshed after a spiritual bath. This bath will make you feel spiritually cleansed, rejuvenated, and ready to take on any challenges. It uses a special ingredient - wine. This beverage is packed with polyphenols, which are potent antioxidants. To truly relax while taking this bath, you can sip a glass of wine while soaking.

Ingredients:

- Essential oils - orange, lemon, sandalwood, and myrrh are best
- 1 glass of wine - plus one more to drink
- Lemon and orange rind
- Cinnamon sticks
- Fresh rosemary
- Dried roses
- Grapefruit juice
- Oregano

Instructions:

1. Fill in your tub with water and adjust the temperature to your preference. Prepare the other ingredients while you wait for the tub to fill up.

2. Add everything to the water (except the wine you'll drink) and stir to combine. If you're using loose, dried herbs, put them in a reusable teabag or cheesecloth to avoid clogging your drain.

3. After soaking for 20-25 minutes, do a good exfoliation to further boost your cleansing from the inside out. The massage will enhance the purification properties of the flowers and the antioxidants.

4. Once you have finished, air dry or gently tap yourself dry with a towel. Don't forget to moisturize after your bath to nourish your skin and seal in all the positive energies you've soaked up from the water.

A Spiritual Bath for Improving Energy Flow

This spiritual bath is designed to boost the energy flow through the entire chakra system. You'll be cleansed of negative energies and restore your physical, mental, and spiritual health. It is a combined approach of relaxation and circulation-boosting, enabling better energy flow.

Ingredients:

- Essential oils - chamomile, juniper, cypress lavender, and lemon are best
- Dead sea salt
- A neutral gel
- Honey
- Exfoliant

Instructions:

1. Fill your bathtub, adjusting the water temperature to your preference. Ideally, the temperature should be around 84,2-100,4 degrees Fahrenheit.
2. Add the essential oils to the bath, followed by gel, honey, and sea salt. Adjust the quantities to your preference.
3. Spend at least 20 minutes soaking and relaxing. Before getting out, do a complete exfoliation, massaging your body. This is key for improving blood, lymphatic, and energy circulation.
4. After getting out of the bath, air dry your body. Once you're dry, apply a nourishing oil to seal in the herbs' cleansing effects.

Bath for Unblocking Your Chakras

A nice, calming bath can do wonders for clearing out obstructions from your chakras. It re-establishes a healthy energy flow and balance in your body, mind, and spirit. For the best effects, it's recommended to take this bath strictly for relaxation purposes. Take a quick shower beforehand if you need to clean yourself, so you can focus on your intent to clear out chakra blockages.

Ingredients:

- Himalayan sea salt
- Colorful flowers - you can use dried and fresh
- Candles
- Essential oils
- Incense (optional)
- Meditation material (sounds, music, guides, etc., optional)

Instructions:

1. Clear all clutter around the bathtub. You need a clean tub without distractions.
2. Fill your bathtub with water. Adjust the water temperature to your preference.
3. While the tub is filling, settle on an intent. For example, you can wish to cleanse all the chakras or one or two blocked chakras causing you problems.
4. Light the candles. If you prefer, you can also burn incense. Prepare the meditation material, if any.
5. Add the oils, salt, and flowers to the water, and stir. When choosing the flowers, use the color corresponding to the chakra(s).
6. Get into the bath and spend 20-30 minutes soaking. Spend this time in silence, listen to a guided meditation or music, or do whatever helps you relax in the bathtub.

Enjoy rejuvenating and stimulating your body, mind, and soul by removing negative energy from your chakras with these spiritual baths.

Chapter 9: Crystal Purification and Protection

Have you ever felt like negative energy is weighing you down, and you can't seem to shake it off? Or maybe you've been in situations leaving you feeling vulnerable and unprotected. There are various methods to consider for cleansing and protection, but have you ever considered the power of crystals and stones? Have you ever held a crystal or stone and felt a sense of calm or energy wash over you? Perhaps you've seen them in a store or online and wondered about their purpose beyond being a beautiful accessory. Crystals and stones have been used for centuries for their spiritual and healing properties, and they can be a great additional tool to your cleansing and protection methods. Each crystal carries unique energy and can help ward off negative energy, absorb it, or transform it into something positive.

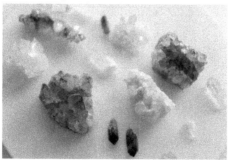

Crystals are powerful tools for cleansing your spirit.
https://www.pexels.com/photo/close-up-of-crystals-6766451/

In recent years, crystals and stones have gained popularity for their ability to aid in cleansing and protection. As life becomes more fast-paced and the surroundings more chaotic, people look for ways to maintain balance and harmony. Crystals can help to achieve this balance. This chapter explores the world of crystals and stones for purification and protection, from amethyst to black tourmaline. Each crystal carries unique energy and can help you on your journey toward inner peace and protection from negative energy. So, delve into the spiritual meanings of each crystal and how they can benefit you in your daily life. With the right crystals, you can create a protective shield around yourself or purify your energy to attract positivity and abundance.

Crystals for Purification

Crystals can be incredibly useful for purification, which involves cleansing negative energy and restoring balance to your life. Here are some of the most popular crystals for purification and their spiritual meanings:

1. Amethyst

Amethyst is a beautiful crystal with a vibrant purple color, known for its powerful energy and ability to promote peace and calm. It has been used for centuries as a tool for spiritual growth, healing, and purification. It's often used to transform negative energy into positive energy, making it a powerful tool for purification. Amethyst is often used to calm the mind, promote clarity, and aid spiritual growth. This beautiful crystal is associated with the crown chakra, the energy center located at the top of the head. This chakra is associated with spiritual connection, enlightenment, and the integration of the mind and body. One of the most common ways to use amethyst is to carry it with you as a piece of jewelry or a small stone in your pocket. Carrying it with you allows you to benefit from the crystal's energy throughout the day. You can place amethyst in your home or workspace to promote peaceful and calming energy.

2. Clear Quartz

Clear quartz is one of the most versatile and popular crystals available. Its clear and transparent appearance makes it known for amplifying and magnifying energy, making it a powerful tool for spiritual growth and transformation. Clear quartz has long been used to purify and cleanse energy. It's often called the "*master healer*" due to its ability to amplify the energy of other crystals, remove negative energy, and promote positivity. Clear quartz is associated with the crown chakra, which enhances spiritual connection, enlightenment, and higher consciousness. It can help balance and harmonize the chakras, promoting overall balance and well-being. Clear quartz can be used in numerous ways to promote spiritual growth and purification. One common way is to place the quartz in a room to promote clarity and positivity. It can be used in meditation to enhance intuition and promote inner peace. Clear quartz is used in energy healing practices, like Reiki, to help balance and harmonize the chakras and promote overall well-being.

3. Rose Quartz

Rose quartz is a beautiful and gentle crystal known for its ability to promote love, compassion, and emotional healing. Its soft pink color is associated with the heart chakra, the energy center located in the chest. This chakra is associated with emotional balance, love, and connection. The rose quartz's purpose is to promote emotional healing and encourage self-love and compassion. It can help release negative emotions and replace them with love and positivity. Rose quartz is believed to have a calming effect on the mind and body, reducing stress and promoting inner peace. One of the most common ways to use rose quartz is by placing it near the bed or under the pillow to promote peaceful and restful sleep. It is often used in meditation to promote emotional healing and self-love. Holding a piece of rose quartz in your hand during meditation can help connect with its energy and promote love and compassion.

4. Selenite

Selenite is a truly unique crystal that stands out from other purifying crystals due to its distinctive properties. One of the most remarkable properties of selenite is its ability to cleanse and purify not only other crystals but also spaces and environments. Selenite is believed to have the power to remove negative energy, blockages, and stagnant energy from the aura and the environment, leaving lightness and clarity. Unlike other crystals, selenite does not need to be cleansed or charged. It's known for its self-cleansing properties and is believed to cleanse and recharge other crystals in its proximity. It can help clear mental fog and promote mental clarity, making it an excellent choice for those seeking greater focus and insight. Selenite is a high-vibration crystal that can help connect to higher realms of consciousness and spiritual growth. It's associated with the crown chakra and promotes spiritual awakening and deep meditation. Selenite helps enhance psychic abilities and intuition, making it a popular choice for those interested in spiritual development and divination.

5. Carnelian

Carnelian is a beautiful crystal prized for its unique properties for centuries. It's believed to have powerful cleansing properties, particularly with the sacral chakra. This energy center is located just below the navel and is associated with creativity, passion, and pleasure. In addition to its ability to purify and cleanse the sacral chakra, carnelian is associated with several other properties. It promotes vitality, courage, and motivation, making it an excellent choice for those seeking to take action and make positive life changes. One of the unique things about Carnelian is its ability to remove creative blockages and promote inspiration and passion. It helps open up the creative energy flow, allowing for greater expression and a deeper connection with the creative self. Carnelian can be used in many ways to promote purification and cleansing. Some people wear carnelian as jewelry, like a necklace or bracelet, to keep it close and promote its unique properties throughout the day. Others place carnelian in a bowl of water to create an elixir ingested for its unique properties.

6. Celestite

Celestite is a stunning crystal that has long been revered for its unique properties. It's believed to have powerful cleansing abilities, particularly for the throat chakra. This energy center is associated with communication and self-expression, and celestite can help remove obstructions and promote clear communication. In addition to its cleansing properties, celestite promotes calm and tranquility. It's associated with the higher chakras, particularly the third eye and crown chakras, associated with intuition and spiritual connection. Many people use celestite in meditation or spiritual practices to promote inner harmony and connection with the divine. It helps remove negative energy and promote well-being, making it an excellent choice for those seeking to promote overall purification and cleansing. You can use it in a crystal grid or place it on your chakra during meditation to promote its unique properties throughout the body.

Crystal Combinations

Several combinations work particularly well when using crystals for purification and cleansing purposes. These combinations are often chosen based on the crystal's specific properties and how they complement and enhance one another. Some examples include:

- **Amethyst and clear quartz:** Amethyst promotes spiritual growth and clears negative energy. Clear quartz amplifies the other crystals' energy and promotes clarity and focus. Together, these two crystals can help remove negative energy and promote inner peace and clarity.

- **Carnelian and citrine:** Carnelian is associated with creativity and vitality, while citrine transforms negative energy into positivity and abundance. Together, these two crystals can help remove negative energy and promote creative flow and abundance.

- **Selenite and rose quartz:** Selenite is associated with cleansing and clarity, while rose quartz promotes love and compassion. Together, these two crystals can help remove negative energy and promote emotional balance and well-being.

- **Citrine and pyrite:** Citrine is known to attract abundance and promote positivity, while pyrite enhances manifestation and promotes success. Together, these two crystals can help amplify your manifestation energy and bring your goals and desires to fruition.

- **Quartz and selenite:** Clear quartz amplifies energy and promotes clarity, whereas selenite cleanses and purifies energy. When combined, these crystals help clear and purify your energy field, leaving you feeling refreshed and revitalized.

Crystals for Protection

Using crystals for protection presents a wide range of options. Every crystal possesses a distinctive energy and unique properties, aiding in building a protective shield around the wearer. Certain crystals excel in safeguarding against negative energy, while others offer physical protection against harm.

1. Black Tourmaline

Black tourmaline is a powerful crystal with properties making it an excellent choice for protection. It repels negative energy and provides grounding and stability to the wearer. This crystal is known for its protection against psychic attacks, negative entities, and other harmful energies in the environment. Incorporating black tourmaline into your life for protection can be done in several ways. One way is to wear it as jewelry, like a pendant, bracelet, or earrings, allowing you to carry its protective properties wherever you go. You can place black tourmaline around your home or workplace to create a protective barrier against negative energy.

When using black tourmaline for protection, keeping it cleansed and charged is important. Placing it in sunlight or moonlight or smudging it with sage or other cleansing herbs helps clear the absorbed negative energy and restore its protective properties. Black tourmaline is particularly effective when used in combination with other protective crystals. For example, combining it with smoky quartz can create a powerful shield against negative energy. It can be used with clear quartz to amplify its protective properties and create an even stronger protective barrier.

2. Citrine

Citrine is a warm and vibrant crystal often associated with prosperity and abundance. However, it has potent protective properties, making it an excellent addition to your protection toolkit. This crystal is known for transmuting negative energy into positive energy, helping create a positivity shield around the wearer. One of the unique properties of citrine is promoting mental clarity and focus. It is particularly useful when dealing with stressful or challenging situations, as it calms the mind and reduces anxiety or overwhelms.

Incorporating citrine into your life for protection can be done in various ways. One of the most effective ways is to carry it with you as a talisman or amulet. It allows you to always access its protective energy, no matter where you are. Citrine can be placed around the home or workplace to create a protective barrier against negative energy. When using citrine for protection, keeping it cleansed and charged is essential. Place it in sunlight or moonlight, or smudge it with sage or other cleansing herbs. Citrine can be used with other protective crystals for even greater effectiveness.

3. Black Jade

Black jade is a powerful crystal known to protect you from negative people and the energies they manifest. This crystal allows you to access your intuition and protect yourself from negative energies and situations. People often find it challenging to pinpoint the source of negativity; black jade is efficient for this purpose. It can help you find the root cause of negativity and protect you and your loved ones. Black jade crystal strengthens the connection to your intuition and gives you heightened awareness. This crystal can help you make decisions for your highest good to navigate life with confidence and clarity. Carry it with you to make the most of black jade's energy and to protect your energy from negativity. It is especially helpful when traveling or embarking on new adventures since the various energies you encounter can be unfamiliar and potentially challenging. To use this crystal in a protective ritual, place the crystal in your hand and set your intention. Keep the crystal in your pocket or wear it as a necklace when you've set the intention. Whether worn as jewelry or kept in your pocket, black jade is a reminder of your inner strength and resilience, helping you face life's challenges with grace and courage.

4. Hematite

Hematite is a protective crystal with unique grounding energy to help shield its wearer from negative influences. This mineral is known for its metallic luster and deep black color, giving it a strong and powerful presence. The purpose of hematite as a protective crystal is to create a barrier between the wearer and negative external and internal energies. It helps keep you grounded and centered, essential for maintaining a strong and protective aura. Hematite has been used for centuries for its protective and grounding properties, making it a popular choice for spiritual and healing practices. Incorporating hematite into your daily life can be as simple as wearing it as jewelry or carrying it in your pocket. Meditating with hematite is a powerful way to connect with its energy and strengthen your aura.

5. Labradorite

Labradorite is a mystical and protective crystal with a mesmerizing play of iridescent colors that catch the light and shimmer like magic. Its unique energy is known to ward off negative energy and protect its wearer from harm. The purpose of labradorite as a protective crystal is to help shield its wearer from unwanted energies trying to penetrate its aura. Its captivating colors calm the mind, making maintaining a positive and protective mindset easier. Labradorite enhances intuition and psychic abilities, making it a popular choice for spiritual practices.

Incorporating labradorite into your daily life can be as simple as carrying it with you as a protective talisman or wearing it as jewelry. Its energy is enhanced by holding it during meditation or placing it on your third eye chakra during a healing session. One of the unique properties of labradorite is its ability to protect and balance the aura, which is especially beneficial for empaths or sensitive individuals easily influenced by the energies of others. It can be used with other protective crystals to create a powerful energy shield.

6. Cat's Eye

Cat's Eye is a fascinating, protective crystal highly regarded for its unique ability to ward off evil and unseen danger. Its name comes from the distinct band of light running through the center of the stone, resembling a cat's eye. The purpose of the cat's eye as a protective crystal is to provide safety and security to its wearer, especially during uncertainty or change. Its energy helps release fear and anxiety, allowing for greater courage and strength in challenging situations. It is a powerful tool for dispelling negative energy and protecting against psychic attacks.

Incorporating the cat's eye into your life for protection can be as simple as carrying it in your pocket or wearing it as jewelry. Like all crystals, it is important to regularly cleanse and charge the cat's eye to maintain its protective properties through smudging with sage, placing it in the full moon's light, or using other preferred cleansing methods.

7. Shungite

Shungite is a powerful and unique crystal believed to have exceptional protective properties. This dark, almost black stone is composed of carbon molecules called fullerenes, known for their ability to neutralize harmful substances and electromagnetic radiation. As a result, shungite creates a protective shield against the negative energy emitted by technology and modern devices. In addition to its protective qualities, shungite has a grounding and stabilizing effect on its wearer. It helps with emotional balance and promotes calm and relaxation, making it a popular choice for protection against stress and anxiety and spiritual practices requiring a clear and focused mind.

Shungite can be used in several ways for protection. It is often worn as jewelry, like pendants or bracelets, or placed in the environment as pyramids or spheres. It is used to create shungite water, which is believed to have powerful healing and protective properties.

Crystal Combinations

Choosing stones that complement each other's properties and energies is essential when combining crystals. Here are some crystal combinations that work well together for protection:

- **Black tourmaline and clear quartz:** Black tourmaline is an excellent stone for protection against negative energy, while clear quartz helps amplify its energy and enhances its protective qualities.

- **Hematite and red jasper:** Hematite provides grounding and protection, while red jasper enhances courage and strength, making it a powerful combination for protection against physical harm.

- **Shungite and pyrite:** Shungite is known for neutralizing negative energy, while pyrite is a protective stone warding off negativity and danger.

- **Citrine and tiger's eye:** Citrine absorbs negative energy and transforms it into positive, while tiger's eye promotes courage, strength, and protection.

As you explore the world of crystals for purification and protection, remember these are tools to support your intentions and inner work. Crystals can help create a harmonious environment and protect you from negative energies, but they are not a substitute for personal responsibility and self-awareness. Take the time to connect with each crystal, learn about its unique properties, and find the ones that resonate most with you. Experiment with different crystal combinations, meditate with and incorporate them into your daily routine. Remember, crystals are powerful allies, and with a little intention, they can help you create a more balanced, peaceful, and protected life.

Only a few crystals for purification and protection have been mentioned in this chapter. Research online or enquire at your local stores and discover the vast availability of crystals.

Chapter 10: Cleansing and Protecting Your Loved Ones

As you journey through life, you will encounter many obstacles and challenges, leaving you feeling spiritually drained and vulnerable. Fortunately, various tools and techniques are at your disposal to help you cleanse and protect yourself from negative energy. But what about the people you care about? Your loved ones are as susceptible to negative energy and spiritual attacks as you. In a world often chaotic and unpredictable, it's natural to want to shield your loved ones from harm and negative energy. This chapter explores ways to extend the protection you've learned to your family and friends so they can feel spiritually safe and secure.

You can apply the methods in earlier chapters to protect others from negative energies; you merely need to modify the techniques to suit, whether a bath for your pets or children or a meditation session to help them find peace and security. The techniques in this chapter are rooted in ancient wisdom and have been used by cultures around the world for centuries. Incorporating them into your daily life, you cultivate peace and security for yourself and your loved ones, no matter what challenges arise. These methods provide unique and powerful ways to keep your loved ones safe and spiritually sound, even when you're not physically with them.

Meditation

Meditation is a powerful way to connect with the divine and release negative energy. With a few modifications, you can use this technique to provide spiritual protection and cleansing for your loved ones. This meditation helps create a protective energy field around your loved ones and promotes peace and positivity.

- Find a quiet and comfortable space where you won't be disturbed. You can sit or lie down, whichever is more comfortable for you. Follow these steps:

- Close your eyes and take a few deep breaths to relax your mind and body. Visualize your loved one standing in front of you, surrounded by a beautiful white light. This light represents their spiritual purity and protection.

- As you visualize the light surrounding your loved one, imagine negative energy or emotions leaving their body and being absorbed by the light. See the light grow stronger and brighter with each breath, cleansing and protecting your loved one.

- Next, take a moment to focus on positive affirmations. Repeat the following phrases silently or aloud, whatever feels most comfortable to you:

    o *"My loved one is safe and protected at all times."*

    o *"Negative energy has no power over my loved one."*

    o *"My loved one is surrounded by love and positivity."*

    o *"My loved one is filled with light and positivity."*

    o *"I radiate positive energy and love to my loved one, strengthening their aura and protecting them from negativity."*

- Take a few deep breaths and continue to visualize the protective cocoon of light surrounding your loved one. Send positive energy and love to them, and know they are protected and safe.

- When ready to end the meditation, take a few deep breaths and slowly come back to the present moment. Take a moment to ground yourself and release the remaining negative energy.

- By using this meditation technique, you provide ongoing spiritual protection and cleansing for your loved ones. It's a simple yet powerful way to promote peace, positivity, and safety.

Candle Ritual

Candle rituals have been used for centuries to promote spiritual cleansing and protection. The best part is they can be performed in person or from a distance, making them versatile for promoting positive energy and warding off negativity for your loved ones. Choose a white or black candle for cleansing and protection. White represents purity and positive energy, while black represents grounding and protection. You can use different colored candles depending on the ritual's intention. Follow these steps:

- If you're performing the ritual in person, find a quiet and comfortable space where you won't be disturbed. Sit or stand in front of your loved one, holding the candle in your hand. Light the candle and visualize your loved one if you're performing the ritual from afar.

- Light the candle, and imagine the flame representing the power of spiritual cleansing and protection. Hold the candle up to your loved one, and imagine the light and energy of the flame flowing into their body and cleansing the negative energy.

- If you're performing the ritual from afar, imagine the candle's light and energy reaching your loved one and cleansing away negative energy.

- Next, you can incorporate positive affirmations to reinforce the ritual's protective energy. Repeat the following phrases silently or aloud:

  o *"I call upon the power of this candle to cleanse and protect my loved one's energy."*

  o *"My loved one is surrounded by a shield of positive energy, protecting them from negative influences."*

  o *"All negative energy is released from my loved one's body and mind and replaced by positive energy."*

  o *"I send love and positivity to my loved one, promoting a healthy and vibrant energy field."*

- Allow the candle to burn for as long as you feel comfortable, focusing on the positive energy exchange between you and your loved one. When ready to end the ritual, take a few deep breaths and slowly release the remaining negative energy.

By using candles for cleansing and protection, you promote spiritual well-being and provide ongoing protection for your loved ones.

Crystal Protection

Crystals can protect in many ways, including creating a protective barrier around your loved ones, enhancing their personal energy field, and promoting safety and security. As discussed previously, some of the best crystals for protection include black tourmaline, amethyst, and clear quartz. Follow these steps to use crystals to protect your loved ones:

- Choose a crystal that resonates with your loved one's energy and intention. Depending on what feels right for them, you can use one or several crystals.

- Hold the crystal in your hand and set your intention for protection. Visualize a protective shield around your loved one or their space.

- Place the crystal in a location where your loved one spends most of their time, such as their bedroom, living room, or office.

- Remind your loved one to connect with the crystal's energy and intention whenever they need protection.

In addition to protection and cleansing, crystals can support your loved ones in many other ways. Here are a few ideas:

- **Meditation**: Encourage your loved one to hold a crystal while meditating to enhance the connection with their inner self.

- **Jewelry**: Giving your loved one a crystal necklace, bracelet, or earrings can give them the crystal's energy throughout the day.

- **Grids:** You can create a crystal grid by placing several crystals in a specific pattern to manifest a particular intention, such as healing, abundance, or love.

- **Bathing:** Add crystals to your loved one's bath to promote relaxation and cleansing.

Smudging

Smudging is a powerful way to protect and cleanse the energy of your loved ones, but you can make it even more personalized by creating a special smudging bundle specifically for them. Follow these steps:

- Gather a variety of herbs and flowers that resonate with your loved one's energy and intentions. You can include sage, rosemary, lavender, rose petals, or other herbs or flowers that hold special meaning for them. You'll need natural string or twine to tie the bundle together.

- Next, take a moment to set your intention for the smudging bundle. Visualize your loved one and imagine them surrounded by a protective shield of positive energy. You can include positive affirmations, such as *"May this bundle protect and cleanse my loved one's energy."*

- Once you've set your intention, assemble the smudging bundle. Take each herb or flower and place it in a pile, holding the intention for your loved one in your mind. Once you have all the herbs and flowers together, wrap them in natural string or twine, tying them tightly to create a compact bundle.

- To use the smudging bundle, light one end and allow it to smolder. You can use a heatproof bowl or shell to catch the ashes. Move the smudging bundle around your loved one's body, fanning the smoke with your hand or a feather.

- When you have finished smudging, extinguish the smudging bundle by pressing it into the heatproof bowl or shell.

Spiritual Baths

Spiritual baths are a powerful way to protect and cleanse the energy of your loved ones, but choosing ingredients safe for sensitive skin is important. Before using new ingredients, it's always best to test a small skin area to ensure no adverse reactions.

- Fill a bathtub or large container with warm water, adding herbs like lavender, chamomile, or calendula for a calming and soothing bath or rosemary and peppermint for an energizing and uplifting bath. You can add Epsom salts or baking soda for an extra cleansing boost.

- For pets, choosing ingredients safe for their skin and fur is important. Avoid using essential oils or ingredients known to be toxic to pets, like tea tree oil. Stick to safe and gentle ingredients like oatmeal, aloe vera, or chamomile.

- For children, choosing ingredients safe for their delicate skin is essential. Avoid using ingredients like strong essential oils that could cause irritation or allergic reactions. Stick to gentle and nourishing ingredients like oatmeal, coconut oil, or lavender.

- Once you've added in your ingredients, invite your pet or child into the bath. As they soak in the water, offer positive affirmations to help them feel protected and cleansed. For example, you could say, *"May this bath protect and cleanse your energy, filling you with peace and love."*

- After the bath, gently pat your pet or child dry with a soft towel and offer them a comforting hug or snuggle. You can smudge the room with sage or palo santo to help clear lingering negative energy.

Protection Jar

Protection jars are simple and effective ways to offer your loved ones ongoing protection and positive energy. Here's how to make one:

Materials:

- Small glass jar with a lid
- Salt or sand
- Herbs and crystals for protection (suggestions: black tourmaline, rosemary, sage, bay leaves, cinnamon, cloves, or lavender)
- Paper and pen
- Optional: ribbon or twine for decorating

Instructions:

1. Set your intention for the protection jar. For example, *"May this protection jar offer ongoing protection and positive energy to my loved ones, shielding them from harm and negativity."*

2. Fill the bottom of the jar with a layer of salt or sand. This creates a base for your herbs and crystals to sit on.

3. Next, add your herbs and crystals. Choose items that resonate with the intention of protection, like black tourmaline for grounding and protection or rosemary for clarity and protection.

4. Write your intention on a small piece of paper and fold it up, placing it inside the jar on top of the herbs and crystals.

5. Close the jar tightly and decorate it with ribbon or twine, if desired.

6. Place the jar in a safe and visible location, like on a shelf or in the corner of your loved one's room. You can carry it with you for added protection.

Whenever your loved ones need extra protection or positive energy, you can hold the jar and visualize the protective energy surrounding them. You can add or remove herbs and crystals to adjust the jar's energy.

Salt Healing

Salt has long been used for spiritual protection, to create an energy shield to repel negative influences, and promote safety and well-being. You can use special sea salt in several ways or other salts for protecting your loved ones:

Materials:
- Sea salt or rock salt
- Small cloth or fabric bag
- String or ribbon

Instructions:
1. Set your intention for salt protection.
2. Place a small amount of sea salt or rock salt in a cloth or fabric bag.
3. Tie the bag closed with a piece of string or ribbon, creating a small pouch.
4. Hold the salt pouch in your hands, focusing on your intention for protection.

5. Visualize a shield of white light surrounding your loved ones, repelling negative energy or influences.

6. Place the salt pouch in a safe and secure location, like on a shelf or under a bed.

7. Hold the salt pouch in your hands whenever you need to renew the protection and repeat the visualization and intention-setting process.

Salt Protection

Salt protection can be a simple yet powerful way to create an energy shield around your loved ones, promoting safety and well-being. Regularly renewing the protection helps keep their energy clear and protected. Another way you can utilize salt protection can include:

Materials:

- Sea salt or rock salt
- Protective herbs of your choice (e.g., rosemary, sage, lavender)
- Small bowl or dish
- Your loved one's photo

Instructions:

1. Choose a space where you will create the salt protection circle. It could be your loved one's bedroom, living room, or another place where they spend a lot of time.

2. Sprinkle a thin layer of salt around the room's perimeter to create a circle. As you do, visualize a bright, protective light surrounding the room and your loved one.

3. Sprinkle the protective herbs into the bowl or dish, and place your loved one's photo in the center.

4. Place the bowl or dish in the center of the salt circle.

5. Close your eyes and visualize a strong, protective energy emanating from the bowl or dish, enveloping your loved one in a protective bubble.

6. When ready, open your eyes and say a positive affirmation.

7. Leave the salt protection circle in place for as long as necessary. You can refresh the salt and herbs as needed.

Protection Talisman

A protection talisman is a great gift for someone who needs to feel safe and secure. You can create a talisman using crystals or other objects associated with protection, like black tourmaline, onyx, or hematite.

Materials:

- A crystal or stone associated with protection
- String or wire
- Small cloth bag or pouch
- Optional: additional protective herbs or symbols

Instructions:

1. Choose a crystal or stone that resonates with protection, like black tourmaline, onyx, or hematite.
2. String the crystal onto a length of string or wire, leaving enough space at the ends to tie the talisman into a loop.
3. You can add other protective herbs or symbols to the talisman if desired. For example, you might include dried sage, rosemary, or a protective symbol like a pentagram.
4. Tie the ends of the string or wire together to create a loop.
5. Place the talisman in a small cloth bag or pouch and give it to your loved one.

Whether you're performing a spiritual bath or creating a protection jar, the intention behind your actions makes them truly powerful. Setting your intentions and working with the right tools creates safety and well-being for those who matter most. Of course, exercising caution and taking safety measures is essential when working with potentially dangerous ingredients like fire and herbs. But with careful research and mindfulness, you can create a beautiful and effective way to protect and cleanse your loved ones.

Glossary of Useful Herbs

Basil

Basil is one of the most versatile herbs for cleansing and protection. It has long been used for its spiritual connections, as many cultures, like the Hindus, believe it wards off bad energy and attracts good fortune. Beyond these beliefs, basil has been prized for its medicinal properties. It helps soothe inflammation, boosts the immune system, and improves digestion. In addition to its physical healing powers, many people use basil in rituals before bed or during gatherings to evoke peace, love, and joy among those present. The possibilities of using basil to boost your physical and mental health are endless. Adding basil essential oils to a warm bath or creating a powerful cleansing spray to spritz around your sacred space. Additionally, basil is safe for children and pets, meaning it's a great addition to many households. Flavor-wise, basil is one of the most popular herbs, adding a delicious kick of flavor to any dish.

Aloe Vera

Aloe vera is an incredibly versatile healing herb and plant with applications ranging from skincare and cosmetics to spiritual practices. It can be used externally to soothe sunburn and keep the skin hydrated, added to bathwater, or boiled as tea. It is even safe enough for children and pets, making it a great natural protective shield against environmental factors and toxins. Aloe vera brings an extra layer of energy cleansing throughout your home when burned in situ like a smudging ritual. Alternatively, you can simply place a pot of aloe vera on one or both sides of your front door to guard your abode. Its flavor also adds something unique to food seasoning - incorporate aloe into your meals for a taste sensation.

Sage

Sage has long been considered a holy, healing herb invested with protective and cleansing properties. Practically, sage is a tactile plant. It can be burned or used as herbal tea and infusions, added to baths for additional cleansing, or used as a seasoning. It's popularly used in households. Small bushels of sage can be kept around the house to promote happiness, keep evil energetics away, and clear negative vibrations. Further, to protect your children and pets from negative influences in the household (as some believe), place a few potted sages around the house. These plants are non-toxic, making them an ideal choice for home protection. Last but not least, sage remains one of the top choices for spiritual practices like smudging rituals due to its purported powers of "positive energy" clearance.

Mint

Mint is one of the most versatile healing herbs and plants. It can be burned, steeped in tea, or as seasoning for food and drinks, but more importantly, it has spiritual meanings, making it a great addition to cleansing and protection rituals. Many believe that keeping mint in your home will bring good luck. Adding a few mint leaves to a pot of water and allowing the aroma to permeate your space is said to ward off bad vibes. Including crushed mint leaves in your bath helps relieve relaxation and muscle pain. Mint essential oil can be applied topically or aromatically. If making tea with fresh mint is your cup of tea (pun intended), it provides important nutrients and spiritual meaning. Finally, if you have pets or small children, keep an eye on interactions with fresh mint plants, as they are more likely to cause reactions than the dried varieties. No matter how you incorporate mint into life for its energetic or physical benefits, you can enjoy its energizing effects any time of the year.

Vetiver

Vetiver, or *Chrysopogon zizanioides*, is an incredible healing herb with numerous benefits if used correctly. This aromatic grass is native to India and South East Asia and has long been valued for its many spiritual, physical, and mental benefits. As a cleansing tool, it can be burned to bring forth positive energy and clarity. It can be brewed in teas to aid relaxation and is an excellent choice for spell work and ritual baths. Suppose you want to keep your home safe from energetic disturbances. In that case, adding vetiver into a potted plant or directly into the earth of each corner of your home can create deep protection. Using vetiver with children or pets, taking extra caution, and diluting the product is important since it is strong in scent but otherwise perfectly safe for all ages. Additionally, many chefs like adding ground vetiver root as a seasoning for its unique herbal flavor.

Lavender

Since ancient times the herb lavender has been prized as a magical plant to enrich life in many ways. It is known for its wonderful scent and healing properties, making it impossible to ignore lavender's strengths. Practically, it can be used for everything from creating soothing oils and cleansers for mental clarity to the trendy popular use of dried lavender blossoms in sachets. It is believed to help with protection and purification spells and can bring good luck when added to charms or carried as crystals. As an added bonus, in small doses or concentrations, lavender is considered safe for children and pets. Whether you add fresh air to your home with lavender essential oils or gently place sachets around your office or home, embrace the cleansing power of this uniquely gifted plant's medicinal and spiritual properties.

Jasmine

Jasmine is a magical and healing herb with origins in ancient history. From the moment you catch its distinct fragrance, you can unlock a range of positive vibes. Several spiritual meanings are attributed to jasmine. These include protection against negative energy, enhanced mental clarity, and amplified love and devotion. Jasmine has numerous practical uses in cleansing and protection:

- You can burn dried jasmine essence in your home to clear the air while bringing in positive energy
- Mix it with lavender for ultimate serenity
- Apply a few drops on your pillow or blankets for restful sleep
- Make an infusion of leaves and drink it to purify your body
- Wear the flower around your neck to benefit from its medicinal properties.

Additionally, jasmine is generally safe for children and pets when used properly.

Thyme

Thyme is a healing and protective herb that has been around for ages. The Greeks of ancient times used it for medicinal purposes. It has a long history in spiritual practices associated with cleansing rituals, luck, and safety. Despite its traditional uses, thyme is still popular in modern life; you can burn it to cleanse a space or make tea. Thyme has numerous practical applications - add it as seasoning to your dishes or put some in a pot as a protective charm. Although thyme is always safe for adults, it should not be used as food seasoning for young children, and pets should be kept away from burning thyme as smoke could irritate their lungs. Thyme offers many wonderful benefits when used correctly.

Rosemary

Rosemary is an incredibly versatile healing herb and plant, used for many cleansing and protecting purposes. It is believed to bring good luck and protection into the home, protect from negative energies, and encourage purification. Besides its practical uses like warding off insects, transforming bathwater into a magnesium-rich soak, tea for headaches, improving breathing, and aiding digestion, it is often burnt as incense or used in charms to concentrate on life's tougher problems. Rosemary oil can be soaked into a cotton ball and diffused around the room. It is safe for children and pets. Other ways include carrying it on you for good luck or wearing it as a crown. Incorporating this ancient herb into your life could bring welcome peace during a time filled with technology overload.

Bamboo

Bamboo is much more than a plant – it's a multi-purpose healer. Carefully harvested and handled, bamboo can be an integral part of your spiritual cleansing routine. Bamboo is thought to absorb negative energy, leaving the space free of unwelcome vibes and protecting the aura from external negative sources. Keep a few stems around your home or office for wealth, good luck, and protection to incorporate bamboo into your practice. Place them in areas of heavy traffic like doorways to ensure everyone entering the home or workspace benefits from its calming energies, or tie seven fresh jade green stalks with a red ribbon and hide it in an out-of-sight corner for powerful protection from the outside world. Additionally, the scent of burning dried bamboo helps create a tranquil atmosphere indoors. Whether you opt for smudging or a loving display, using this mysterious healing plant definitely won't harm children or pets as long as you exercise caution when handling burning materials.

Peace Lily

Peace lilies (Spathiphyllum) are a beautiful addition to many homes and gardens. Many people do not realize that peace lilies are herbs and plants with healing qualities, perfect for cleansing and protection. Spiritually, peace lilies can help bring security, inner stillness, and harmony. Practically, these herbs and plants have a unique ability to rid an area of negative energies or generate positive vibes when used in ritual spells.

Usage tips include:

- Infusions made from the flowers or leaves for drinking.
- Use fresh sprigs over yourself or others for spiritual cleansing.
- Carrying the dried petals in a pouch to ward off bad luck.
- Peace lilies are safe for children and pets, but purchase them from reputable stores or nurseries to ensure they're organic, unprocessed, and grown without synthetic fertilizers or pesticides.

Eucalyptus

Eucalyptus is a healing plant with supernatural properties. Its spiritual meanings rest in its purifying, protective, and cleaning abilities, making it a must-have for your ritual practice. Burning it creates a fuller, stronger connection with the spirit realm. Practically, it's beneficial for potent aromatherapy and reducing anxiety or stress. Eucalyptus is generally safe for children and pets, but parental supervision is recommended due to the heat and vapors. If its consumption is desired, please consult an herbalist before seeking alternate ways of ingesting this powerful plant.

Conclusion

Spiritual cleansing is a journey toward inner peace and purity. It is a process of letting go of the negative energies holding you back and opening yourself up to the positive and healing energies existing within and around you. The path to spiritual cleansing is neither a one-time event nor easy. It is a continuous journey requiring patience, dedication, and a willingness to let go of the past to make room for the future.

The core of spiritual cleansing is that people are made up of energy, which can become blocked or stagnant over time. Negative experiences, emotions, and thought patterns can cause these blocks, manifesting in physical, emotional, and spiritual dis-ease. Engaging in practices and rituals to help release the negativity and reconnect with your true self is essential for clearing these blocks and restoring balance.

The journey toward spiritual cleansing begins with a willingness to examine your beliefs and behaviors. It requires an honest assessment of what is holding you back and a commitment to making positive changes. This process can be challenging, as it often involves facing difficult truths about yourself and your life. However, only by acknowledging and addressing these issues can you begin to move toward a place of healing.

You will encounter obstacles and challenges as you navigate the path toward spiritual cleansing. You may find old thought patterns and behaviors difficult to break, or that negative emotions crop up at the most unexpected times. However, perseverance and a commitment to your spiritual growth will make you stronger and more connected to your true self.

Remember, the process of spiritual cleansing is unique to each individual. There is no one-size-fits-all approach, and what works for one person may not work for another. You must find the practices and rituals that resonate with your soul and make them a regular part of your routine. With each step forward, you will shed layers of negativity and embrace the light within.

The journey toward spiritual cleansing is not easy, but it is a journey well worth taking. You restore balance and harmony to your energy by engaging in practices and rituals to help you release negativity and connect with your true self. This process will not happen overnight, but with dedication and patience, you can transform your life from the inside out. So, let this book serve as a guide and a source of inspiration as you continue your journey toward spiritual purity and enlightenment.

Here's another book by Mari Silva that you might like

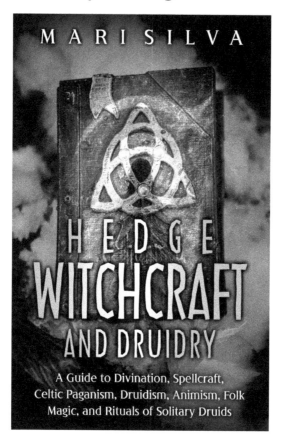

Your Free Gift
(only available for a limited time)

Thanks for getting this book! If you want to learn more about various spirituality topics, then join Mari Silva's community and get a free guided meditation MP3 for awakening your third eye. This guided meditation mp3 is designed to open and strengthen ones third eye so you can experience a higher state of consciousness. Simply visit the link below the image to get started.

https://spiritualityspot.com/meditation

References

(N.d.). Beadage.net. https://beadage.net/gemstones/uses/purification/

(N.d.). Nataliemarquis.com. https://nataliemarquis.com/how-to-sense-energy-for-healing/

(N.d.). Yogainternational.com. https://yogainternational.com/article/view/what-are-the-7-chakras/

"11 Signs You Need A Spiritual Detox & How to Make It Happen." 2015. Mindbodygreen. July 6, 2015. https://www.mindbodygreen.com/articles/signs-you-need-a-spiritual-detox.

10 easy ways to cleanse your home of negative energy. (2012, April 3). Mindbodygreen. https://www.mindbodygreen.com/articles/how-to-cleanse-your-home-of-negative-energy

6 crystals to protect yourself from toxic people & negative energy. (2020, February 11). Mindbodygreen. https://www.mindbodygreen.com/articles/crystals-for-protection

Anahana. (2022, September 1). How to unblock chakras in A few easy steps. Anahana.com. https://www.anahana.com/en/wellbeing-blog/how-to-unblock-chakras?hs_amp=true

Beabout, L. (2022, May 26). Good vibrations: Your complete guide to chakra meditation. Greatist. https://greatist.com/health/chakra-meditation

Bryant, M. (2022, June 13). 25 crystals for charging and cleansing your energy. Sarah Scoop. https://sarahscoop.com/25-crystals-for-charging-and-cleansing-your-energy/

Chapter 4 - moving into higher vibrations. (n.d.). Meditation Guide - Happiness Meditation.

Chee, C. (2021, September 27). 6 of the best crystals for protection: Meaning & how to use. Truly Experiences Blog; Truly Experiences. https://trulyexperiences.com/blog/crystals-for-protection/

Cho, A. (2015, June 17). How to smudge your house to invite positive energy. The Spruce. https://www.thespruce.com/how-to-smudge-your-house-1274692

Choice, C. (2020, August 18). 10-minute practice to ground, breathe, soothe. Mindful; Mindful Communications & Such PBC. https://www.mindful.org/10-minute-meditation-to-ground-breathe-soothe/

Christopher. (2015, September 13). Reiki Level 1 Training: What to expect and how to prepare. Chakra Meditation Info. https://www.chakrameditationinfo.com/reiki/reiki-healing/reiki-level-1-guide-to-reiki-practice/

Clarke, Gemma. 2022. "What Is Spiritual Cleansing? + the Top Cleansing Rituals to Improve Your Energy Field." The Yoga Nomads (blog). Julien. September 24, 2022. https://www.theyoganomads.com/spiritual-cleansing/.

Curtis, L. (2021, September 29). 10 healing herbs with medicine benefits. Verywell Health. https://www.verywellhealth.com/healing-herbs-5180997

D'costa, M. (2012, November 21). Smudging and how it helps to cleanse your aura. Times Of India. https://timesofindia.indiatimes.com/life-style/home-garden/smudging-and-how-it-helps-to-cleanse-your-aura/articleshow/12866742.cms

Elkhorn, V. (2019, December 12). Smoke cleansing as an appropriate alternative to smudging. The Alchemist's Kitchen. https://wisdom.thealchemistskitchen.com/smoke-cleansing-as-an-appropriate-alternative-to-smudging/

English, M. (2018, April 24). Healing plants you should surround yourself with. Martha Stewart. https://www.marthastewart.com/1527900/healing-plants-for-your-home

Estrada, J. (2020, March 6). 5 reiki principles you can use to create more ease and flow in your life. Well+Good. https://www.wellandgood.com/reiki-principles/

Everything you've ever wanted to know about the 7 chakras in the body. (2009, October 28). Mindbodygreen. https://www.mindbodygreen.com/articles/7-chakras-for-beginners

Feldmann, E. (2019, February 7). How to use crystals for protection at home. Penguin.co.uk. https://www.penguin.co.uk/articles/2019/02/how-to-use-crystals-for-protection-at-home-hausmagick

Ford, Debbie. 2018. "Is It Time to Take a Spiritual Cleanse?" Oprah.com. June 8, 2018. https://www.oprah.com/inspiration/is-it-time-to-take-a-spiritual-cleanse.

Fosu, Kimberly. 2022. "3 Signs You Need a Spiritual Detox Plus Ways to Do It." ZORA. January 18, 2022. https://zora.medium.com/3-signs-you-need-a-spiritual-detox-immediately-plus-ways-to-do-it-f8ecc9bbbf98.

Girdwain, A. (2019, April 14). Summon your inner strength and confidence with these powerful crystals for protection. Well+Good. https://www.wellandgood.com/crystals-for-protection/

Gleisner, E. (2002). Reiki. In Principles and Practice of Manual Therapeutics (pp. 175–183). Elsevier.

Haria, D. (2021, August 26). Spiritual Bath: Meaning, Rituals, Techniques, Benefits and More. F and B Recipes. https://fandbrecipes.com/spiritual-bath/

Haugen, D. (2021, February 10). A Ritual Bath For Balancing The Chakras. Mindbodygreen. https://www.mindbodygreen.com/articles/balance-your-chakras-with-a-ritual-bath

Heidi. (n.d.). Smoke cleansing around the world. Mountainroseherbs.com. https://blog.mountainroseherbs.com/smoke-cleansing

How to Raise Your Vibration By Sabrina Reber. (n.d.). How to raise your vibration. Blogspot.com. http://howtoraiseyourvibration.blogspot.com/2011/03/actively-meditating.html?m=0

https://link.springer.com/article/10.1007/s10902-011-9286-2

Humphreys, K. (2019, August 14). Chakra Visualisation. Com.au; Head & Heart Mindfulness. https://www.headandheartmindfulness.com.au/blog-items/chakravisualisation?format=amp

IARP. (2014, April 20). History of Reiki: Read about the origin and traditions of Reiki. IARP. https://iarp.org/history-of-reiki/

Jain, R. (2019, June 13). Complete guide to the 7 chakras: Symbols, effects & how to balance. Arhanta Yoga Ashrams. https://www.arhantayoga.org/blog/7-chakras-introduction-energy-centers-effect/

Jain, R. (2022, December 22). How to unblock chakras with meditation and affirmations. Arhanta Yoga Ashrams. https://www.arhantayoga.org/blog/how-to-unblock-chakras-beginners-guide/?utm_source=google&utm_medium=cpc&utm_campaign=16771375909&utm_content=&utm_term=&gclid=Cj0KCQiArsefBhCbARIsAP98hXSkoM5bTDFkXuDwWKURDcvyTDJrs42d8nocO4aLCBSzZO_PVGkfDlcaAtiGEALw_wcB

Johnson, C. (2021, July 6). Chakra meditation: Unblock the 7 chakras with guided meditation. Anahana.com. https://www.anahana.com/en/meditation/chakra-meditation?hs_amp=true

Judith, A., & White, A. (2022, March 18). The complete guide to the 7 chakras for beginners.

Kalra, P. (2022, August 20). Repeat these 5 principles of Reiki daily for your mind, body and soul. Healthshots. https://www.healthshots.com/mind/happiness-hacks/reiki-for-mind-5-principles-you-must-affirm-everyday-for-mental-strength/

Kurt. (2017, July 4). Finding your centre: Grounding meditation techniques. Earthing Canada. https://earthingcanada.ca/blog/grounding-meditation-techniques/

Kyteler, E. (n.d.). How to make A protection jar (ingredients & spell). Eclecticwitchcraft.com. https://eclecticwitchcraft.com/how-to-make-a-protection-jar-ingredients-spell/

laura. (2020, April 3). 3 incredible spiritual baths rituals to do at home during the quarantine. Hotel CoolRooms Palacio Villapanés Sevilla. https://coolrooms.com/palaciovillapanes/en/3-incredible-spiritual-baths-rituals-to-do-at-home-during-the-quarantine/

Lawrenson, A. (2017, September 3). Chakra meditation: The secret to feeling more calm and grounded? Byrdie. https://www.byrdie.com/chakra-meditation

Lieber, A. (n.d.). How to tell if your chakras are blocked and how to unblock them. Dailyom.com. https://www.dailyom.com/journal/how-to-tell-if-your-chakras-are-blocked-and-how-to-unblock-them/?aff=91&ad=1&utm_source=google&utm_medium=cpc&utm_campaign=PerformanceMaxUK&acct=9358138875&cur=gbp&campaign_id=17483841340&gclid=Cj0KCQiArsefBhCbARIsAP98hXRWn-q_X091H7X4ZcIgx6gY-PFd_sQd0aVthUlimGZyUyUZ1dcDzTUaAq0lEALw_wcB

Lieber, A. (n.d.). The 7 major chakras: What you need to know and how to work with them. Dailyom.com. https://www.dailyom.com/journal/the-7-major-chakras-what-you-need-to-know-and-how-to-work-with-them/?aff=91&ad=1&utm_source=google&utm_medium=cpc&utm_campaign=PerformanceMaxUK&acct=9358138875&cur=gbp&campaign_id=17483841340&gclid=Cj0KCQiA6LyfBhC3ARIsAG4gkF-_3FfS2jnc4id0bCiuycfcP_FYwo2hOBaq5r1Powt2Q7LPTFnvQKEaApEIEALw_wcB

Lisa, P. (2020, February 3). Art of meditation. The Art of Living Retreat Center. https://artoflivingretreatcenter.org/blog/everything-you-need-to-know-about-meditation/

N.d. Yogabasics.com. https://www.yogabasics.com/connect/yoga-blog/spiritual-cleansing/.

Nine-herb home protection talisman. (2015, November 11). Wiccan Spells. https://wiccanspells.info/nine-herb-home-protection-talisman/

Nortje, A. (2020, July 1). 10+ mindful grounding techniques (incl. Group exercise). Positivepsychology.com. https://positivepsychology.com/grounding-techniques/

Paul, N. L. (2016, March 27). Reiki for dummies Cheat Sheet. Dummies. https://www.dummies.com/article/body-mind-spirit/emotional-health-psychology/emotional-health/reiki/reiki-for-dummies-cheat-sheet-209093/

Prasetyo, F. (2022, May 15). How to raise your vibration: The ultimate guide on raising your vibe –. Lifengoal. https://lifengoal.com/how-to-raise-your-vibration/

Raypole, C. (2021, May 5). Metta meditation for mother's day.

Regan, S. (2022, April 26). How To Make Your Bath A Spiritual Experience: 16 Tips & Techniques. Mindbodygreen. https://www.mindbodygreen.com/articles/spiritual-bath

Reiki self-treatment. (n.d.). Cleveland Clinic. https://my.clevelandclinic.org/health/treatments/21080-reiki-self-treatment

Safa Water. (n.d.). Salt Water Bath: A Cleansing, Healing, And Nourishing Ritual For Your Mind And Body. Linkedin.Com. https://www.linkedin.com/pulse/salt-water-bath-cleansing-healing-nourishing-ritual-your-mind-

Smudging 101: Burning sage to cleanse your space & self of negativity. (2015, March 13). Mindbodygreen. https://www.mindbodygreen.com/articles/smudging-101-burning-sage

Stelter, G. (2016, October 4). Chakras: A beginner's guide to the 7 chakras. Healthline. https://www.healthline.com/health/fitness-exercise/7-chakras

The 3 levels of reiki: What are they & what do they mean? (2014, December 1). Mindbodygreen. https://www.mindbodygreen.com/articles/the-3-levels-of-reiki

The three degrees of reiki. (n.d.). Reiki-light.uk. https://reiki-light.uk/the-three-degrees-of-reiki/

Top 15 spiritual plants. (2020, December 24). Floweraura Blog. https://www.floweraura.com/blog/plants-care-n-tips/top-10-spiritual-plants

What are chakras? (n.d.). WebMD. https://www.webmd.com/balance/what-are-chakras

What is a Spiritual Bath, and Do I Need One? - Black Female Therapists. (n.d.). Blackfemaletherapists.Com. https://www.blackfemaletherapists.com/what-is-a-spiritual-bath-and-do-i-need-one/

Your guide to candle magic. (n.d.). Rylandpeters. https://rylandpeters.com/blogs/health-mind-body-and-spirit/your-guide-to-candle-magic

Yugay, Irina. 2022. "Eliminate Problems from within Using Spiritual Cleansing." Mindvalley Blog. November 25, 2022. https://blog.mindvalley.com/spiritual-cleansing/.

Zoldan, R. J. (2020, June 22). Your 7 chakras explained – plus, how to tell if they're blocked. Well+Good. https://www.wellandgood.com/what-are-chakras/amp